TOBACCO, TRUSTS, AND TRUMP

How America's Forgotten War Created
Big Government

JIM RUMFORD

Copyright © 2018 by James C. Rumford, Jr.

All rights reserved. No part of this book may be reproduced in any form or by any means—electronic, mechanical, photocopying, scanning or otherwise—without written permission from the author, except by a reviewer who may quote

Brooksville Press

Publisher's Cataloging-In-Publication Data

Names: Rumford, Jim.
Title: Tobacco, trusts, and Trump: how America's forgotten war created
   big government / Jim Rumford.
Description: [Miamisburg, Ohio]: Brooksville Press, [2018] | Includes
   bibliographical references.
Identifiers: ISBN 9781732710405 | ISBN 9781732710412 (ebook)
Subjects: LCSH: Tobacco industry--United States--History. | United
   States--Politics and government. | Working class--United States--
   History. | Militia movements--United States--History. | Social
   conflict--United States--History.
Classification: LCC HD9135 .R86 2018 (print) | LCC HD9135 (ebook) |
   DDC 338.1/73710973--dc23

Printed in the United States of America

Contents

Introduction: What They Don't Want You to Know	1
Chapter 1: "You've Never Worked a Day in Your Life"	5
Chapter 2: The Buck Stops with Buck Duke	20
Chapter 3: Night Riding	35
Chapter 4: United States v American Tobacco Co.	46
Chapter 5: When Government "Helps"	56
Chapter 6: Populists, Socialists, and the Taxes They Love	68
Chapter 7: Filling the Swamp	80
Chapter 8: When the Little Guy Stands Up for Himself	96
Chapter 9: The Ultimate Anti-Establishment Career Path	110
Chapter 10: Domestic Enemies	121
Chapter 11: Great Again	139
Chapter 12: More Work to Be Done	155
Conclusion: What's the Future?	170
About the Author	175

Dedication

To my Aunt Jo Ann and Uncle Tom Kinney, Custodians of the Family's Tobacco Wars Document Collection.

Introduction
What They Don't Want You to Know

A lawless militia of ten thousand masked men roam the city streets and country roads of the United States of America.

Brandishing firearms, they terrorize cities and farms all across the heartland, set fire to warehouses and barns, destroy millions of dollars of product, and tear businessmen from their homes in dead of night to horse-whip them until they bleed out.

Because they're mad as hell. Mad about corporate greed. Mad about wages and incomes plummeting while profits and shareholders' value soar. Mad about the American Dream being ripped from their working class fingers. And mad about a corrupt government that won't do anything about it.

Counting farmers, lawyers, preachers, doctors, and statesmen among their members, this paramilitary force is no posse of unemployed, entitled Millennial misfits. These untrained civilian-soldiers consider themselves Patriots. But as American blood soaks American soil, they insist that the end justifies the means.

This may seem like the opening scene of a futuristic post-Apocalypse Sci-Fi movie. It's not. It's history, *American* history, and it happened in the heartland of America over one hundred years ago—Kentucky, Tennessee, Ohio, Indiana, Arkansas, West Virginia, the Carolinas. In what was the most violent and prolonged conflict between the nation-splitting Civil War and the terror-ridden Civil Rights struggles of the 1960's, a little-known war changed the course of our history—and our economy.

Between 1904 and 1910, the Tobacco Wars consumed what coastal elites call "the flyover states." From Durham, North Carolina to the foothils of Kentucky, anti-Establishment citizens banded together to form the Night Riders—a vicious mob of vigilantes who saw it as their place (and their right) to enact justice on those who took advantage of them. An eye for an eye, a livelihood for a livelihood.

I am a witness to this history, which most Americans know nothing about. Both sides of my family fought in the Tobacco Wars, one a Night Rider; the other, his victim, a tobacco businessman selling to the Tobacco Trust. While you will find every cited

WHAT THEY DON'T WANT YOU TO KNOW

source noted at the end of each chapter, I haven't put pen to paper to explore only the past.

This book needed to be written because the United States of America is carelessly, blindly careening towards the same chaos that gave rise to the Night Riders—and their enemy, the monopolies and trusts within American industry. A hundred years ago, integrity-free tycoons obliterated businesses and jobs, crushed hopes and dreams for a better life, and upended local economies all across America. Their fortunes grew as a result.

Today, these patterns of history are repeating themselves. The stage is set for a new breed of Night Riders to undertake a scorched earth campaign, motivated by anti-One Percent, anti-Big Government sentiments.

I hope I'm wrong, but history's patterns are undeniable. So think of this book as a warning. A warning of what can—no, *probably*—will come to pass over the coming decades in part as a result of the circumstances surrounding the great populist uprising that was the 2016 Presidential Election. From Silicon Valley technology oligopolies to the meteoric rise of the TEA Party, from the packed-like-sardines crowds of Bernie Sanders supporters to the wickedly easy outsourcing of America's blue collar careers, today's headlines are echoing those of a century ago.

I know something about those headlines—my family's estate has one of the largest collections of primary source Tobacco Wars documents in the United States. Over the next twelve chapters, a bloodstained story of heroism and greed will unfold, a story that *they* don't want you to know about. By the final page, you'll know why—and you'll know who, exactly, "they" are.

When I was five years old, I overheard my grandfather accuse my grandmother's father of destroying his own father's tobacco barns—and his dignity—in a single night.

"No he didn't! My father was a good man, and I'll not hear another word of it," my grandmother snapped at him.

But I knew the truth. He was right.

I share this anecdote because I am now my grandfather, and the United States of America is my grandmother. By writing this book, I am telling the truth. Truth suppressed by the textbooks, ignored by politicians, and scoffed at by intellectuals.

Will you, like my grandmother, give me a proverbial slap across the face by venting your cognitive dissonance in a one-star review? Or will you take history—American history—seriously?

Either way, it's still true. History that many Americans have been denied from learning for over a century is coming to light, and I have all the sources to back it up.

This chapter's opening scene happened in American history. Twelve chapters from now, you'll realize it can happen again—unless we do something about it.

Chapter 1
"You've Never Worked a Day in Your Life"

If there's one thing we need more of in this country, it's work ethic. Gone are the days when children learned the value of labor by working alongside their parents or elders in the family business, on the farm, in apprenticeships, or at after-school jobs. Nowadays, a lot of kids channel their energy into sports and afterschool activities. That's a good thing.

Inner city kids, on the other hand, are not participants in sports—or in a work ethic. In cities like Chicago, dropping out of school, using drugs, and joining gangs go hand in hand.

We have two separate cultures, one that values hard work and one that doesn't. Inner city youngsters have lost sight of our history and the place that strong work ethic had in making ours the greatest country and economy on the planet.

I know I'm not the only one who can say how glad I am that I didn't have those drug and crime culture distractions as kids do now. Like many in

TOBACCO, TRUSTS, AND TRUMP

my generation, as soon as we were old enough to read and write and our feet could reach the pedals of a truck or tractor, we got to work. In my case, that work took the form of entrepreneurship at age ten.

The business partner: my grandfather. The place: Bracken County, Kentucky. The product: Tobacco.

"If you haven't raised a crop of tobacco, you've never worked a day in your life," Grandpa Rumford always said. I'm convinced the latter half of that sentence is true for our Leftist friends, but even the average hard-working middle class professional has no idea how much labor is required to turn a tobacco seed into a Lucky Strike.

As far back as I can remember, I spent summers and weekends on my grandparents' farm feeding the chickens, shucking corn, and helping out in the tobacco patch. Those early years of work were basically an apprenticeship that earned me the responsibility of my own patch.

Grandpa Rumford made an agreement with his neighbor over a one-tenth of an acre plot on his small farm. "Let me and the boy farm it, and we'll split the profit two ways." A handshake later, the sharecropping deal was done.

At ten years old, I helped carry on a tradition that dates back to the first Native American tobacco smokers hundreds of years ago.

"YOU'VE NEVER WORKED A DAY IN YOUR LIFE"

After hitching a plow to a horse, my grandfather and I plowed the soil of the ten foot by fifty foot tobacco bed. After the plowing came disking, followed by sterilizing. To do this, we set the soil on fire by dragging burning logs hitched to a horse across the bed. To anyone unfamiliar with this process, we looked like a couple of pyromaniacs trying to spark a forest fire.

We weren't the only ones burning soil. If we'd been able to fly over this region at night, we would've seen hundreds of small fires all across the Kentucky landscape.

Tobacco is a fragile seed. If we didn't do everything just right at every step, we wouldn't even have the chance to start over.

Once the black smoldering soil cooled off, we prepped it further with rakes longer than I was tall, hoed the tobacco bed and sowed the seeds one handful at a time. By the time seeds met soil, we had invested over two hundred hours on the project without earning a single penny.

After planting the seeds, we laid a cotton bedding sheet over the bed. Once the first sprouts of green emerged after a month or so, I gently slid a wooden board on each side and across the tobacco bed to make picking the plants easier. One by one, I pulled up the plants, roots and all, careful not to step on any of them. We pulled up as many plants in one day as we could set by sundown that same day.

TOBACCO, TRUSTS, AND TRUMP

To the back of his horse, my grandfather hitched a rolling two-seat platform with a water container secured to the top and a plow-like blade to the bottom. This was our tobacco setter; the process of tobacco setting began.

As the horse trudged across our one-tenth of an acre plot, the plow ripped open the soil and the container dripped water into the open earth. I then took one of our tobacco plants and placed it into the newly watered spot in the open soil. The tobacco setter then moved the earth back around it. Over and over and over we did this, moving at the speed of a few yards per hour, until every last tobacco plant had its place in the plot.

"If you haven't raised a crop of tobacco, you've never worked a day in your life."

The tobacco started to grow over the weeks that followed, but our battle with nature hadn't even begun. Soon, the weeds appeared. We used horses with a cultivating plow to turn the dirt and remove them one at a time. As the next round of weeds grew—these taller than the previous—we used hoes by hand because the tobacco was too tall to use a tractor or horses. I got quite good at doing this without damaging the plants, especially after deweeding the entire tenth of an acre three times.

Next came the worms, emerging from the soil around the tobacco stalks to feast on each leaf. With my bare hands, I checked every single inch of ev-

"YOU'VE NEVER WORKED A DAY IN YOUR LIFE"

ery single plant and squished the worms between my thumb and forefinger as I went. At dinner time, which we today call lunch, we washed our hands in hot water from a wood burning stove.

If you've ever raised vegetables in a backyard garden, you know what a hazard suckers can be, especially on tomatoes. These tiny stems emerge like urban welfare addicts at a federal entitlements office, funneling nutrients to themselves that should've gone to the rest of the plant.

Going leaf by leaf, I pruned each tobacco plant of its suckers by hand. When the flower bloomed at the top of the of the plant, it was time for harvest.

To go from a tobacco plant to a tobacco product, I first broke the flower off the top of the stalk (called topping the plant) and let it sit for a few days. I then had to chop off the tobacco stalk at its base. I did this with a sharpened tomahawk. Then, I stood a spear-tipped stick upright into the ground and impaled the freshly chopped tobacco stalks onto this stick for easier transport—six tobacco stalks per stick.

If we did everything right—and we did—the harvest was bountiful. After letting them wilt for a day or two in the field, we loaded the tobacco sticks onto a horse-drawn wagon or a tractor, then backed the wagon or tractor into my grandfather's barn.

From there, we had two choices for hanging the tobacco. I could climb to the fourth level of my grandfather's barn to hang the tobacco sticks from the top tier and shake the dirt from them. But it was about one hundred and thirty degrees up there, or so it felt.

As an alternative, I could stay on the ground floor of the barn and hang the tobacco sticks, where I would be covered from head to foot in dirt that fell from the tobacco sticks thanks to the other harvesters hanging the sticks above me.

By mid October or November, the tobacco stalks cured into a brown case-like color. That was our signal; time for the stripping room. There, we slid the six tobacco stalks off each stick, stripped each stalk of its leaves, separated the three grades of tobacco one leaf at a time, and hand-tied these leaves together in small bundles with another tobacco leaf.

Next, I slid these brown leaf bundles together back onto the tobacco sticks and laid them under a hand press to compress them, which took a few hours. Careful to keep the three grades of tobacco separate, we then laid the now-pressed tobacco into tobacco baskets for travel to its final destination—the tobacco warehouse to be sold at auction.

Three hundred and one dollars.

After my grandfather's neighbor took his share, I had one hundred and fifty dollars—roughly one thousand three hundred today, accounting for inflation.

Since I could buy a fresh pair of Levi's for only two dollars and forty-nine cents, my share was noth-

"YOU'VE NEVER WORKED A DAY IN YOUR LIFE"

ing to sneeze at. Imagine if I had invested my earnings into gold instead! At roughly thirty-five dollars an ounce then—and almost one thousand four hundred today—my farming reward could have purchased gold worth over six thousand dollars today. What is it they say about hindsight?

But compared to most tobacco farmers, I had it easy. A few years back, I met my then-girlfriend's father for the first time. He had risen from a poor tobacco farming background to president of a dairy company.

"Where you from, son?"

"Dayton, sir." We addressed our elders with respect in those days. "But originally, Bracken County, Kentucky."

"Bracken County, eh? So you're one of those rich Bracken County tobacco farmers, aren't you?" For a moment, I thought I saw sadness in his eyes. "You had it EASY! You didn't have to raise all that tobacco by hand like we did, did you?"

We raised tobacco by hand. He says we didn't. What is he talking about?

The sunburned summer before my eleventh birthday was no picnic. I shrugged off his comment and gave no reply.

Many years later, I met with the supervisor of a local wastewater treatment plant outside of Dayton. The city needed the kind of erosion corrosion protection products that we sell at Rumford Industrial

TOBACCO, TRUSTS, AND TRUMP

Group. After the meeting, we retired to the lunchroom for a chit-chat.

"Where you from?" the supervisor asked me. By his relaxed drawl, I could tell his own answer to that question would be somewhere near the Mason-Dixon line.

"I live in Dayton, Ohio. But me, my family, and grandparents are all from Bracken County, Kentucky," I said.

"Oh, you're one of those rich Bracken County tobacco farmers, aren't you? Y'all had it easy, didn't you? We had to raise tobacco by hand."

What the hell is he talking about? I thought. Since no pretty ladies were up for grabs this time around, I spoke my mind.

"What the hell are you talking about?" I hoped this unfiltered response wouldn't damage the deal. After all, the treatment plant needed my products, not my professionalism.

"I bet you had tractors or horses when you raised tobacco, didn't you? I bet you had a horse to pull the plow, didn't you?"

"Well..." I felt like I was youngster again, cross-examined by a superior. "Yeah. Yeah, I did."

"We didn't have any of that." The supervisor looked away. "Me and my brother went out to our folks' tobacco bed, we had to take a shovel to turn over the soil and then rake it by hand instead of using a plow and disk with a horse like you did. Then

"YOU'VE NEVER WORKED A DAY IN YOUR LIFE"

we had to pull fiery logs across the soil with chains by hand. No horses. We didn't have a tobacco setter with water dispensers like you did. We had to fill two five-gallon buckets with water at the creek at a time. My brother had a spade to dig a hole, I put the plant in, and he poured a little of that water into the soil. After getting rid of the weeds, worms, and suckers by hand as you did, then harvesting the crop, we had to pull the wagon ourselves out of the barn, up to the field, then back to the barn. No horse, no machinery of any kind for any of it. That's what you call raising tobacco by hand. That's how we did it in Morgan County. You had it easy over there in Bracken. You didn't have to raise tobacco by hand like we did, did you?'"

With this conversation informing the previous one from many years earlier, I finally realized something. *I* was the one who hadn't worked a day in his life—not compared to these Morgan County farmers, at least. Even in the 1950's, one of the hardest, dirtiest jobs I could have ever done was relatively easy compared to tobacco farming *without* Grandpa Rumford's modern tools.

Now, let's do this; rewind the clock back a hundred and fifty years from modern times. The United States stitched itself together after being torn apart by civil war. Brother turned against brother, father against son, friend against friend, State against State.

TOBACCO, TRUSTS, AND TRUMP

In four short years, two percent of the population was annihilated by bullet and disease.[1] If a war on that scale occurred today, we'd be burying six and a half million people. Could our civilization handle that? Somehow, we did then. But the outlook of Reconstruction-era America was still bleak for Confederate veterans especially and southern tobacco farmers in particular.

Before, during, and after General William Tecumseh Sherman's March to the Sea, Union soldiers did their best not only to punish the Confederates, but humiliate them. City after city, farm after farm, home after home, Union soldiers looted before setting everything ablaze.[2] If you've ever seen the infamous image of New York City on 9/11 taken from the International Space Station, with those two dark clouds of smoke and ash visible from miles above earth, you have a pretty good idea of what much of Kentucky, Tennessee, Virginia, Georgia, and the Carolinas would have looked like from above in 1865.

After General Robert E. Lee surrendered to General U.S. Grant at Appomattox Court House, thousands of southern farmers-turned-soldiers-turned-farmers again came home...to nothing. Years of backbreaking manual labor in their fields, wasted. The majority of southerners didn't own slaves, so whatever they could produce with their own two hands was their sole income source.[3]

"YOU'VE NEVER WORKED A DAY IN YOUR LIFE"

Now that you know how difficult, time-consuming, and even *painful* raising a small crop of tobacco is, imagine how much harder it would have been for ex-Confederate tobacco farmers a century and a half ago, with their morale stolen and their farms destroyed.

Tobacco had made its way between Confederate and Union soldiers during spontaneous trade truces like the one depicted in Ted Turner's film *Gods and Generals*, so southern tobacco farmers at least had a growing market of northern tobacco product buyers. Still, tobacco farmers had to rebuild in order to meet this demand after the Civil War. Imagine opening up a store but you have nothing to sell to the line of customers filling up your lobby.

"Reconstruction" was the perfect title for this period of American history, but not every ex-Confederate farmer started over with nothing. East of the Smoky Mountains in the Piedmont region of North Carolina, a forty-four year-old farmer, father, and former slaveholder dragged himself home to his forsaken farmland.

In April of 1865, George Washington Duke found himself a prisoner-of-war of the Union army. A parole and one hundred and thirty-four miles later, he made his way back to the family homestead on foot.[4] Like most of his countrymen, Washington Duke expected to come home to nothing but a wife and children—if they were even alive.

TOBACCO, TRUSTS, AND TRUMP

They were. So was something else—hope. Though Washington Duke had to sell all of his tobacco farming equipment to provide for his family before conscription into the Confederate Navy, his five barns of tobacco remained untouched by Union plunderers.[5] A miracle, by definition.

Because he had all the supply but no means to acquire more of it, Washington and his sons Benjamin and James—the latter son known as "Buck"—gave up tobacco farming in favor of manufacturing. W. Duke and Sons was born, a corn crib acting as their first factory.[6]

This entrepreneurial pivot put the Duke family on the fast track to financial freedom and fortune. Most tobacco farmers were happy to grow tobacco on a few acres per year and sell it for cash money every winter. Knowing how many blisters my fingers got in the first week of working a tobacco bed, I wholeheartedly agree with their decision.

What began as a decade of problems for the south ended as a decade of profit for the Dukes. Growing consumer demand from as far away as Europe gave Washington Duke the funds he needed to build a warehouse on his property, followed by an even larger facility in the up-and-coming city of Durham.[7,8] While tobacco farmers all over America's heartland sold product by the pound for a couple of nickels each, the Dukes owned an empire in-the-making.

As the last decade of the bloodiest century in

"YOU'VE NEVER WORKED A DAY IN YOUR LIFE"

world history so far came to a close, the Duke patriarch handed the reigns of the company to his younger and business-savvier son Buck. A socialite and schemer with an eye for the ladies—and the affection his fortune could earn from them—Buck decided to test out a fairly new business model that steel tycoon Andrew Carnegie used to dominate his own industry, "Vertical Consolidation."[9] Even if this term doesn't ring a bell, most people have heard of the result of Vertical Consolidation—monopoly.

Forming the American Tobacco Company after his father's retirement, Buck Duke proved that a leafy green plant could become as profitable as Carnegie steel, Rockefeller oil, or Vanderbilt rail. While his family's former competitors, the humble tobacco farmers and sharecroppers, were content to see the price of tobacco soar past twelve and then fifteen cents a pound, Buck Duke focused on expanding his influence in the industry.

By acquiring one company after the next in the tobacco industry, Buck "consolidated" his business operations into a single "vertical." In a few years, he built a monopoly the same way the notorious "Robber Barons" did, buying out the competition in order to pay for goods and services at cost, not wholesale or retail prices. This drove profits up while pulling down the price for delighted consumers.

After purchasing a license to install the world's first automated cigarette rolling machine in his fac-

TOBACCO, TRUSTS, AND TRUMP

tories, Duke saw his cost of producing cigarettes drop to one-sixth of what it had been.[10]

Meanwhile, thanks to advertising's influence on pop culture, holding a cigarette became as American as baking an apple pie. Duke's American Tobacco Company—soon known to insiders as the "Tobacco Trust"—prepared itself to meet that need. By 1900, the Tobacco Trust controlled ninety-three percent of the United States cigarette market.[11]

That's a problem. When supply of a product rises, demand for it surges, and the cost to produce the product to meet the demand plummets, what happens?

It's basic economics. My generation witnessed the phenomenon happen with the computer—digital data storage, specifically. In 1980, you could pay a company called Morrow Designs to store twenty-six megabytes of data for roughly five thousand dollars.[12]

Do the math on that, and the bill for a single gigabyte of data comes to two hundred thousand dollars. Almost forty years later, any joker off the street with a five-dollar bill can buy a flash drive at Walmart to safely store *sixteen* gigabytes. What only multi-millionaires could afford when I was a young salesman, the general public can easily and inexpensively access today.

While the price for a pound of tobacco didn't decrease *that* drastically when the Tobacco Trust's shadow loomed over turn-of-the-century America, the effects of Vertical Consolidation were more catastrophic than any Futurist could have predicted.

Notes:

1. "Civil War Casualties." Civil War Trust. Accessed December 21, 2017. https://www.civilwar.org/learn/articles/civil-war-casualties.

2. Nelson, Megan Kate. "Urban Destruction during the Civil War." *Oxford Research Encyclopedias: American History*, June 2016. Accessed December 21, 2017. doi:10.1093/acrefore/9780199329175.013.313.

3. Pruitt, Sarah. "5 Myths About Slavery." History. May 3, 2016. Accessed December 21, 2017. http://www.history.com/news/history-lists/5-myths-about-slavery.

4. Durden, Robert F. *The Dukes of Durham: 1865-1929*. Durham, North Carolina: Duke University Press, 1975. 7-13.

5. Durden, *The Dukes of Durham*

6. Durden, *The Dukes of Durham*

7. Prince Jr., Eldred E. *Long Green: The Rise and Fall of Tobacco in South Carolina*. Athens, Georgia: University of Georgia Press, 2000. 49.

8. "2.7 The Dukes of Durham." 2008. Accessed December 21, 2017. http://www.learnnc.org/lp/editions/nchist-newsouth/4418.

9. Brandt, Allan M. *The Cigarette Century: The Rise, Fall, and Deadly Persistence of the Product that Defined America*. New York, New York: Basic Books, 2007. 36.

10. Chandler A.D., Jr. *The Visible Hand: The Managerial Revolution in American Business*. Cambridge, Massachusetts: Harvard University Press, 1977.

11. Freddoso, David. "James Duke Smoked 'Em Out To Dominate Tobacco Arena." Investor's Business Daily. January 4, 2016. Accessed December 21, 2017. https://www.investors.com/news/management/leaders-and-success/james-duke-hit-it-big-in-tobacco/.

12. Komorowski, Matthew. "A history of storage cost." Mkomo.com. September 8, 2009. Accessed December 21, 2017. http://www.mkomo.com/cost-per-gigabyte.

Chapter 2
The Buck Stops with Buck Duke

My Great-Grandfather George Washington Kinney was a good man. The kind of guy you wanted to help out when he needed it because you knew he'd do the same for you. Ex-President Barack Hussein Obama had men like him in mind when insulting us hardworking midwesterners for clinging "to guns or religion."[1]

Great-Grandpa Kinney had both, thank you— a New Testament in his pocket and a Smith and Wesson on his belt. Like my Grandfather Rumford, George Washington Kinney made an honest living in part by raising a healthy crop of tobacco year after year. He was also a tobacco buyer. That meant, he bought tobacco from farmers who didn't have tobacco barns to house their tobacco. He would hire them to get the crop ready for market. In his barn were housed thousands of pounds of tobacco.

THE BUCK STOPS WITH BUCK DUKE

In the days before running water, electricity, and gasoline engines, life was hard. Farming was harder. While your average turn-of-the-century metropolis witnessed the dawn of these transformative amenities, Bracken County, Kentucky wasn't quite there yet. If you needed help, there was no telephone to call the police. Telegraph messages were an option if you could afford them and had the patience of a saint. But if you couldn't and didn't, you'd better hop in the saddle and hope like hell your horse's legs could get you where you need to go before it's too late.

On a breezy summer night in 1905, George Kinney chose that option. In a scene straight out of a Spaghetti Western, Great-Grandpa Kinney strode up to the United States Army encampment on the rugged green hills of Maysville, Kentucky, armed with enough firearms to satisfy a Doomsday Prepper.

"They've threatened me! Can I count on your protection?" he told a young Lieutenant. George Kinney's reputation as a hardened, self-reliant man preceded him. Whatever threat this was, had to be taken seriously.

"Did they show up after sundown? With switches?" The Lieutenant asked, well aware of the enemy's tactic of terrifying their chosen victims before following through on the threat.

"In the dead of night." I imagine my Great-Grandfather gave a Clint Eastwood-esque nod. An

TOBACCO, TRUSTS, AND TRUMP

Ennio Morricone track would have been appropriate for the conversation.

"You ain't been selling to the Trust, have you?" The Lieutenant certainly knew the answer. The enemy's hordes only appeared on the outskirts of your farm brandishing weapons of torture if you broke the agreement among tobacco farmers—sell tobacco to the Trust at *their* price, and you're as good as dead.

"Yes, I have. But a man's got a right to earn his own living. No boycott will help me do that. I've got a tobacco crop to tend and a family to feed. With the price a pound of tobacco can fetch going down all over, I don't have time for nonsense. Are you gonna help me or ain't you?" Based on family diaries from the time, I know that's what he would have said to the Lieutenant.

"Let me see what I can do."

The United States Army agreed to send a platoon to protect the Kinney farm—for an entire year. Each day and every night, soldiers patrolled the property, from the land bordering the old national highway, Highway 10, just outside Brooksville, Kentucky, to the family barn with its bountiful harvest of tobacco ready to be sold to an American Tobacco Company-owned buyer.

But nobody came. One year to the day after my Great-Grandfather's plea, the Lieutenant gave up the wild goose chase.

"Whoever they were, I reckon those men surely ain't coming back."

THE BUCK STOPS WITH BUCK DUKE

With no good arguments to force an extended stay, George Kinney let them leave without protest. He shouldn't have.

That very night, the torches of a lawless cavalry appeared on the edge of the Kinney farm.

Flung from his slumber by the screams of hired hands fleeing for their lives, my Great-Grandfather looked out his bedroom window. Countless musket barrels were pointed at his homestead.

Surrounded.

No escape.

"George Washington Kinney! Show yourself!" A shrill voice cried out like a demon beckoning a poor soul to suffer eternal punishment.

This voice didn't belong to a monster, but to an embittered farmer who'd lost everything to the great Tobacco Trust—George Washington Jett, a different Great-Grandfather of mine.

Great-Grandpa Kinney alerted his still-sleeping wife, a fiery redhead named Eliza Jane. With a snarl and a spit, he muttered two words with a disgust usually reserved for cussing.

"Night Riders..."

I've always wondered why America's most popular party game among families is named after monopolies. Sure, it can be fun to rack up a fortune, amassing one imaginary property after the next and sending your opponents to jail. In the real world, a monopoly is not child's play. The word itself is derived from Latin, *monopōlium*, which refers to owning an exclusive right to sell a product or service.[2]

Common sense might tell you that consumers are the primary victims of monopolies, but if you recall from Chapter 1, when the cost to produce a good decreases drastically, so does retail price. That's probably why a journalist and publisher named John Moody wrote so favorably about Buck Duke's American Tobacco Company in his 1904 tell-all book *The Truth about the Trusts: A Description and Analysis of the American Trust Movement*.

In the following excerpt from the book—which is overflowing with ten dollar words, I'll admit—Moody describes how Buck Duke's tobacco business slowly but surely evolved into a monopoly.[3] These events are the prequel to the opening scene of this chapter. (All emphasis in the excerpt is mine.)

> The element of monopoly is comparatively light in the Tobacco Trust, and its stability and success up to the present time have been due quite largely to the fact that its promoters have from the beginning recognized this lack of a strong monop-

THE BUCK STOPS WITH BUCK DUKE

oly element and have seen that they would inevitably be forced to do one of two things: either to **progressively absorb all competition as rapidly as it might spring up, until they finally controlled the tobacco production of the world**, or else succumb to open competition from all corners...

The latter course, however, while more conservative, was the least inviting...therefore **the resolve was doubtless made early in the history of the Trust to progressively reach out and control the entire industry, buying in competitors as rapidly as they might spring up and become formidable.** That this policy, so bold and venturesome, has, up to the present day, succeeded so well, is a living testimonial to the genius of **the remarkable group of men who stand at the head of this wonderful aggregation of consolidated industry**. The Tobacco Trust to-day stands out as a shining example of the adherence to an ambitious, bold, aggressive policy in modern finance, which, up to the present time, **appears to have reaped marked success**...

TOBACCO, TRUSTS, AND TRUMP

> By steady, progressive steps, now covering a period of fourteen years, **it has gradually taken unto itself all that is important or profitable in the tobacco and its allied industries.**
>
> At the beginning, **in 1890, the Trust controlled only 8 plants**, and its capitalization was but $25,000,000. At the present writing [1904], **it has acquired, in all, more than 150 different plants**, and the outstanding capitalization of the various corporations which comprise the Trust is in excess of $500,000,000.[4]

In between the Microeconomics lessons there, you probably noticed how head-over-heels in love John Moody was with the nineteenth century Trusts, just like the corrupt mainstream media is with Left-wing political candidates today.

A "shining example," "remarkable," "bold," "ambitious," "marked success?" Really? Get a room, John.

Opinions aside, let's dig into a few of the phrases and sentences I bolded. If you're not a history buff yet, you will be by the end of this chapter.

> *"...progressively absorb all competition as rapidly as it might spring up, until they finally controlled the tobacco production of the world..."*

THE BUCK STOPS WITH BUCK DUKE

Like I hinted at in Chapter 1, this is exactly what Buck Duke did after his father Washington gracefully exited W. Duke and Sons. Within a few decades of its founding, the American Tobacco Company acquired countless competitors, a move that allowed this new Trust to produce over a hundred brands of cigarettes, over sixty percent of smoking and chewing tobacco, nearly eighty percent of snuff tobacco, and fourteen percent of all cigars in America.[5] In that short amount of time, David—Washington Duke—was replaced by Goliath—his son, Buck.

> *"...the resolve was doubtless made early in the history of the Trust to progressively reach out and control the entire industry, buying in competitors as rapidly as they might spring up and become formidable."*

By 1900, tobacco tycoon Buck Duke's vision to control "one of the first great holding companies in American history" had materialized.[6] He had plenty of help. Notice how this next excerpt from Moody's book cites not an individual, but a shadowy group of investors behind the scenes.

"...the remarkable group of men who stand at the head of this wonderful aggregation of consolidated industry... appears to have reaped marked success."

TOBACCO, TRUSTS, AND TRUMP

There's that word again—consolidation. So who exactly is the group of men John Moody is referring to? At the very beginning of the book, he tells us.[7]

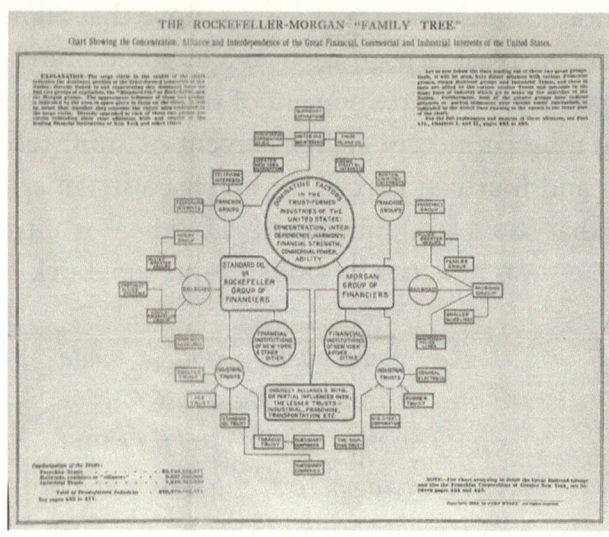

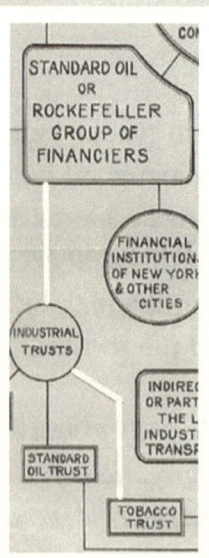

THE BUCK STOPS WITH BUCK DUKE

Each of these circles and squares represents a Trust in American industry, from steel and copper to natural gas and smoking tobacco. As the "blown up" view below reveals, the Man Who Built America—John D. Rockefeller—and his investor pals were in cahoots with Buck Duke, financially enabling him to make the tobacco industry his personal profit playground. (White lines are drawn for emphasis.)

Because every conspiracy theorist reading this is salivating so much they need a spittoon, I devote Chapter 8 to exposing the bastardized relationship between the One Percenters shown in Moody's pictograph and their Big Government allies. For now, note that while the buck stopped at Buck Duke in the tobacco industry, many other players were involved in his rise to fame and fortune. You might say they played a game of Monopoly® with every intention to control every street and every property on the board.

The last part of that Moody quote is the most important, at least on paper. (Pun intended.)

> *"...in 1890, the Trust controlled only 8 plants, and its capitalization was but $25,000,000. At the present writing [1904], it has acquired, in all, more than 150 different plants, and the outstanding capitalization of the various corporations which comprise the Trust is in excess of $500,000,000."*

TOBACCO, TRUSTS, AND TRUMP

There are quite a few definitions for capitalization, most of which require an MBA to understand. Let's define it simply as the amount of capital—investments, assets, shares of stock, etc.—controlled by a single entity.[8] In this case, the entity was Buck Duke's Tobacco Trust.

Within fourteen years of the American Tobacco Company being listed on the New York Stock Exchange, the amount of wealth under Buck Duke's control had increased by a factor of *twenty*. Like President Donald J. Trump said about winners and losers, it's all about how you respond to what life throws at you.[9] The Dukes saw a gap in tobacco manufacturing, and they filled it.

But where there's a winner, there's a loser. Based on the story of the tobacco industry you've read so far, you know who lost—the farmer. The man in the tobacco beds pulling logs, squeezing worms, and hacking stalks. Farmers like my Great-Grandfathers George Washington Kinney and George Washington Jett. Once that first domino—vertical consolidation—fell on all the others in the industry, there was no stopping the consequences.

When I raised my first crop of tobacco, the final stop for the cured leaf bushels was the warehouse auction block. There, multiple buyers could bid one after the other, netting sharecroppers, farmers, and landowners a rewarding profit.

THE BUCK STOPS WITH BUCK DUKE

A half-century prior to my tobacco venture, the outlook was worse than bleak. When there was only one company to place a bid—Duke's American Tobacco Company—what happened to the average selling price of a pound of tobacco? Down it went from twelve cents per pound to as low as one penny.[10,11]

To say this caused a problem is the understatement of my life. All across America's heartland, farmers sold their crops at auction for less than the cost to produce them.[12] In other words, "ignorant, illiterate" tobacco farmers—as one journal at the time called them—found themselves paying the Tobacco Trust to take product off their hands.[13] It goes without saying that you should not be paying customers; they should be paying you!

Four years into this BS, somebody decided to do something about it—a Kentucky plantation owner by the name of Felix Ewing. On September 24th, 1904 in the western Kentucky city of Guthrie, just a few miles north of the Tennessee border, Ewing gathered a crowd of over six thousand irate farmers, their destitute wives, and their hungry children.[14] Their message was the same as every rebellion, every uprising, every revolution throughout human history—*"It's time to fight back!"*

Ewing's audience welcomed his plan with the enthusiasm of a parched desert traveler stumbling upon an oasis:

TOBACCO, TRUSTS, AND TRUMP

Step one, stop selling tobacco to Buck Duke or anyone affiliated with the Trust. *Period*.

Step two, wait for the now-limited supply to force the price of tobacco back up.

Step three, sing Hallelujah when the American Tobacco Company agrees to pay farmers a fair price for theri tobacco.

Step four, end the seller's boycott and usher in a utopian era of prosperity for every tobacco field, farmer, and family in the United States.[15]

What impoverished planter could say no to this proposal? Without much opposition, Ewing and his comrades officially formed the Dark Tobacco District Planters' Protective Association of Kentucky and Tennessee—the Planters' Protective Association, or PPA, for short.

I say without "much" opposition for a reason. What about the farmers who *could* afford to sell a few hundred pounds of tobacco to Buck Duke and make a profit—like my Great-Grandpa Kinney?

Every guerilla army in history knows the drill. Start with terror, then add torture. Instant compliance.

To transform a demoralized crowd of tobacco farmers into a ruthless force whose reputation merited a cry for help from the United States Army, the PPA needed help. So they went to the experts, a group of paramilitary rascals who knew a thing or two about comply-or-die tactics—the Ku Klux Klan.

THE BUCK STOPS WITH BUCK DUKE

Notes:

1. Pilkington, Ed. "Obama angers midwest voters with guns and religion remark." *The Guardian*. April 14, 2008. Accessed December 26, 2017. https://www.theguardian.com/world/2008/apr/14/barackobama.uselections2008.

2. Lewis, Charlton T., and Charles Short. *A Latin Dictionary*. Oxford: Clarendon Press, 1879.

3. Moody, John. *The Truth about the Trusts: A Description and Analysis of the American Trust Movement*. 1st ed. Moody Publishing, 1904.

4. Moody, *The Truth about the Trusts*.

5. Armentano, D.T. "Antitrust History: The American Tobacco Case of 1911." Foundation for Economic Freedom. Accessed December 26, 2017. https://fee.org/articles/antitrust-history-the-american-tobacco-case-of-1911/.

6. Porter, Patrick G. "Origins of the American Tobacco Company." *Business History Review*, 1969. Accessed December 26, 2017. https://sites.duke.edu/collardwexler/files/2015/01/origins-of-american-tobacco-company.pdf.

7. Moody, *The Truth about the Trusts*.

8. "Capitalization." Investopedia. Accessed December 26, 2017. https://www.investopedia.com/terms/c/capitalization.asp.

9. Trump, Donald J. Twitter. September 20, 2014. Accessed December 26, 2017. https://twitter.com/realdonaldtrump/status/513252073727873024?lang=en.

10. Cunningham, Bill. *On Bended Knees: The True Story of the Night Rider Tobacco War in Kentucky and Tennessee*. Kuttawa, Kentucky: McClanahan Publishing House, 1983.

11. Nall, James O. *The Tobacco Night Riders of Kentucky and Tennessee, 1905-1909*. Kentucky Bicentennial Edition 1792-1992. Kentucky: McClanahan Publishing House, 1991.

12. Saloutos, Theodore. "The American Society of Equity in Kentucky: a recent attempt in agrarian reform." *The Journal of Southern History*, 1939.

13. Matthews, John L. "Agrarian Pooling in Kentucky." *Charities and The Commons*, May 2, 1908, Volume 20.

14. Matthews, "Agrarian Pooling in Kentucky."

15. Campbell, Tracy. *The Politics of Despair: Power and Resistance in the Tobacco Wars*. Lexington, Kentucky: The University Press of Kentucky, 1993.

Chapter 3
Night Riding

"Warfare Against the Trust To Be Waged Relentlessly By Tobacco Growers...Fire Losses at Russellville Estimated at $100,000...'Night Riders' Take Possession of Trains and Locomotives..."[1]

"Masked And Heavily Armed 'Night Riders' Continue Raids in Kentucky. Many Tobacco Barns Are Reduced To Ashes."[2]

"Panic in Forty-Two Kentucky Counties. Riders Murder Farmer. Preparing for Exodus from the State."[3]

"Bands of Armed and Masked Men Roaming the Country...State of Outlawry Is Increasing in Burley District."[3]

"Federal Troops; Martial Law. Demand To Be Made On Governor [Augustus] Willson...Executive To Call On The President To Send United States Troops To Kentucky."[5]

"Tobacco Valued at $30,000 and Owned by Agents of 'Trust' Was Burned...Homes Destroyed and Lives Threatened, State Official Investigating."[6]

"Prominent Farmer Indicted On the Charge of Night Riding...The grand jury late yesterday afternoon returned

an indictment against [J.M.] Weaver, accusing him of being a member of the larger band of night riders that raided Hopkinsville...and destroyed property valued at several hundred thousand dollars, besides shooting up the city..."[7]

"Night Riders Expected To Attack Murray...Armed Bands Have Terrorized County...Clash Seems Imminent..."[8]

"Alleged Leader Now In Jail...Suspects Fleeing County."[9]

"Riders Attack Homes. Twenty-five Masked Men Dig Up Tobacco Beds, Fire Into Homes and Use Lash on Grower—Boulders Hurled Through Windows."[10]

"Night Riders Are Busy In Pendleton County. Whip One Grower and Destroy Tenant's Tobacco and Do Damage on Another Farm."[11]

"Farmer Wants Soldiers to Guard His Home. Declares Band of 'Night Riders' Visited His Farm."[12]

Today's press tends to inflate news that doesn't matter while downplaying news that does. At least newspapers of a century ago tried their damndest to tell the truth. Between 1904 and 1910, that truth was the fire and fury currently overtaking farms across the American heartland—and no one had a clue how to stop it.

The headlines that begin this chapter appeared on the front pages of newspapers during the war raging across tobacco country. The lawless militia known for "Night Riding" attacked farms and the

NIGHT RIDING

farmers themselves, including my great-grandfather. As the headlines hint, the Night Rider ritual began with abduction of their victims—tobacco farmers selling to the Duke Trust. Forcing the victim's family to watch, the Night Riders strung up the farmer from a tree near their home, horse-whipped the poor man until blood and flesh coated the ground below, then dragged him behind their horses as they galloped through town. This was a brutal warning not to cross the Protective Planters Association and break the boycott of Buck Duke.[13,14] If we connect the dots of history, we know where these horsemen found inspiration for their cruelty.

When Felix Ewing got sick, a farmer and country doctor by the name of Dr. David Amoss from Cobb in Caldwell County, Kentucky took his place at the top of the PPA.[15] Like Leon Trotsky and Vladimir Lenin during the Red Terror brought on by the Bolshevik Revolution, Ewing and Dr. Amoss were the brain and the brawn behind the wave of attacks later dubbed the Tobacco Wars. While Ewing discussed the ideas of the boycott, Dr. Amoss put bullets behind it. So much for the Hippocratic Oath.

To learn how to execute effective campaigns of violence and terror and to maintain secrecy in all his dealings, Dr. Amoss rode down to Nashville to meet with the neighborhood Klansmen.[16] Given the Leftist KKK's reputation for setting the progress of racial tolerance back a hundred years, Dr. Amoss wanted to implement the Klan's tactics. He ended up using KKK passwords himself during private PPA conversations.[17]

Of course, the KKK—originally known as the "Kuclux Clan"—was controlled by and worked to benefit Democrats, as historian Eric Foner noted thirty years ago.[18] This is a fact despite what Leftist activists masquerading as college professors will tell you.

To be politically incorrect, Dr. Amoss wanted to know how the Ku Klux Klan terrified, tormented, and tortured black people. Whatever they were doing, Dr. Amoss figured, it worked. Ideal tactics to borrow to terrorize tobacco farmers breaking the boycott.

Because Dr. Amoss had been a cadet and drillmaster at the military school in Hopkinsville, Kentucky, he knew he'd have no problem training his recruits. But when you throw the so-called "rules of civilized warfare" out the window for the causes of economic and social justice, you have to replace them with something.

Yet while Dr. Amoss and his Night Riders built a brotherhood of vengeance, Buck Duke could not have cared less. This fact is surprising given the Riders' outright hostility towards him, his family, and his businesses. If *you* had an army of armed anarchists ten thousand strong who were willing to destroy as much property and as many lives as necessary to get your attention, wouldn't you be a little worried?

NIGHT RIDING

This was not the case for Buck Duke. The man's impenetrable business model prepared him to defeat the Night Riders' antics. While PPA members kept every pound of tobacco they could get their hands on under lock and key, Duke enjoyed such a surplus of cheap tobacco going back to the 1890's that he had very few problems meeting demand. Even if every privately owned tobacco barn and warehouse went up in smoke—which many of them did—the long-term consequences would be nominal.[19]

Of course, if you're a Liberal economist, you're convinced that disaster and destruction are a fine way to grow the economy. If someone vandalizes a window in your house, you have to buy a replacement and hire a handyman. According to guys like Paul Krugman, that vandal just stimulated the economy![20] I wonder what Krugman would say about the hurricanes that hit Houston and Puerto Rico in 2017.

The predecessor to Krugman's Broken Window Fallacy was the Burned Tobacco Barn Fallacy, apparently. The masked men on horseback hoped to restore their standard of living. Success, however, was limited.

The case of the Night Riders perfectly illustrates why the vast majority of insurgency movements throughout history fail to achieve their primary objective, from pitchfork-wielding Communist farmers and severed head-carrying French peasants to Palestinian suicide bombers and Black Lives Matter property looters. These sorry excuses for humanity have no understanding of reality, the repercussions of their actions, or how unsustainable their tactics are. The Russian farmers starved to death thanks to the Communist central planners they put in power. The French Revolutionaries paved the way for the bloodthirsty ambitions of Emperor Napoleon. Child-murdering Islamofascists motivated the US to send Israel better weapons to defend themselves. BLM and their Antifa allies proved to American voters why Donald J. Trump belongs in the White House for eight years.

The Night Riders of the Protective Planters Association turned tobacco farmers from the victims, into the villains. They "proceeded to organize secret bands, first to threaten [non-members of the PPA], next to destroy his property, finally to whip him, and if need were, to kill him."[21]

From 1904 through 1908, Dr. Amoss goaded his men to trash their consciences—and every town they visited. Humiliating farmers and burning barns no longer satisfied them.[22] As the potential success of their efforts dropped to probably one in a hundred million, they got sloppy.

After discharging their weapons into every structure on main street, the Night Riders planted dynamite at tobacco processing factories they suspected of selling to the American Tobacco Company.[23] During a raid in Hopkinsville where Dr. Amoss'

NIGHT RIDING

men blew two manufacturers sky high, the Riders then descended upon the local jail, dragged the prisoners out of the cells, and lynched them from the tree outside.[24,25]

After these tobacco farmers first saw the price of their product start to dip, they probably had no idea that a few short years later, they would be willing to commit such atrocities.

Based on the population of the tobacco states, I've calculated that more than six hundred and sixty thousand people were directly affected by the masked men on horseback. The headlines of the day proved it to anyone paying attention. Millions and millions of dollars, thousands upon thousands of jobs, and priceless human lives, gone. For what? Yes, thirty-five thousand farmers stopped planting tobacco by 1908, bumping the price per pound up a bit from the pre–Night Rider price.[26] But how many dollars and cents are human lives and livelihoods worth?

In April 1908, the Kentucky National Guard gave the Protective Planters Association a taste of their own medicine. Led by Lieutenant Newton Jasper Wilburn—soon promoted to Captain for efforts worthy of war hero status—the National Guard raided one PPA leader's home after the next. If only cameras from the TV show *Cops: Caught in the Act* could have been there to record it all. Hauled away in chains, Night Riders found themselves threatened with decades of prison time—or worse—if they refused to talk. So they did. Naming names and giving up locations, jailed PPA members brought down the organization they forfeited all integrity and honor to build, from within.[27,28]

While the Night Riders threatened loss of property and possibly life for anyone who broke the Trust boycott, the National Guard offered military protection to citizens who ratted out the Riders. There's a lesson on human nature there somewhere.

Two years into a calculated move to dismantle the Night Riders, America's finest restored law and order to the land by filling our country's jails with these barn-burning terrorists. What surprises me the most about the protracted aftermath of the Tobacco Wars was how few of the Night Riders ended up facing prosecution.

In a classic case of getting the wrong man, our justice system turned a legally blind eye to the atrocities of the Night Riders. Dr. David Amoss, for example, found himself hauled in front of the Christian County Court. Chock it up to pity if you like; the Court let Dr. Amoss go without suffering the consequences of his actions.[29]

Who is easier to scapegoat—a man with money who might be guilty, or a man without money who definitely is?

Despite the morality of capitalism and the lasting progress it offers every society that embraces it, free markets take the blame for every

NIGHT RIDING

problem we face nowadays. So do the top beneficiaries, the capitalists.

This isn't a new trend. What's happening today happened then, over a hundred years ago when the last Night Riders laid down their arms and returned to their farms for good.

And it happened on the most consequential stage on earth—the United States Supreme Court.

Notes:

1. "Warfare Against the Trust To Be Waged Relentlessly By Tobacco Growers. Peace Conference Proves an Utter Failure. Fire Loss at Russellville Estimated at $100,000. 'Night Riders' Take Possession of Trains and Locomotives—Kentucky's Governor Acts." *The Cincinnati Enquirer*, January 4, 1908.

2. "Marked And Heavily Armed 'Night Riders' Continue Raids in Kentucky. Many Tobacco Barns Are Reduced To Ashes. Hundreds of Shots Fired, But No One Is Hit. Governor Wilson Is Asked To Increase Rewards Offered." *The Cincinnati Enquirer*, March 15, 1908.

3. "Panic in Forty-Two Kentucky Counties. Riders Murder Farmer. Preparing for Exodus from the State." *The Courier-Journal*, 70. No. 70. March 21 1908.

4. "Panic in Forty-Two Kentucky Counties," *The Courier-Journal*.

5. "Federal Troops; Martial Law. Demand To Be Made On Governor Wilson. Petitions To Be Prepared Requesting Executive To Call On the President To Send United States Troops to Kentucky. Governor Says Power Does Not Rest With Him...Legislature Can Act." *The Courier-Journal*, March 23, 1908.

6. "...Police Guards at Night for Cincinnati Warehouse Prevent Possibility of Repetition of Covington Fire." *Cincinnati Times-Star* 70. No. 74. March 26, 1908.

7. "J.M. Weaver Arrested. Prominent Farmer Indicted On the Charge of Night Riding." *The Courier-Journal*, March 28, 1908.

8. "...Rush Militia To Calloway. Night Riders Expected To Attack Murray. All-day On Horses From Hopkinsville. Armed Bands Have Terrorized County. Clash Seems Imminent." *The Courier-Journal*, April 3, 1908.

9. "Alleged Leader Now In Jail. Another Arrest Made By Troops at Murray. Joseph Bell Received Papers From Prisoners. Importance Attached To Documents Found On Men. Suspects Fleeing County." *The Courier-Journal*, April 11, 1908.

10. "Riders Attack Homes. Twenty-five Masked Men Dig Up Tobacco Beds, Fire Into Homes and Use Lash on Grower—Boulders Hurled Through Windows." *The Cincinnati Post*, May 5, 1908.

11. "Night Riders Are Busy In Pendleton County. Whip One Grower and Destroy Tenant's Tobacco and Do Damage on Another Farm." *The Louisville Evening Post*, August 1, 1908.

12. "...Asks Governor for Protection. Farmer Wants Soldiers to Guard His Home. Declares Band of 'Night Riders' Visited His Farm." *The Kentucky Bromley-Erlanger*, September 26, 1910.

13. McCulloch-Williams, Martha. "The Tobacco War in Kentucky." Edited by Albert Shaw. *The American Review of Reviews*, February 1908. Accessed December 27, 2017. https://books.google.com/books?id=MigIAQAAIAAJ&pg=PA129&lpg=PA129&dq.

14. Nall, James O. *The Tobacco Night Riders of Kentucky and Tennessee, 1905-1909*. Kentucky Bicentennial Edition 1792-1992. Kentucky: McClanahan Publishing House, 1991.

15. Soodalter, Ron. "Terror in the Night." *Kentucky Monthly*. Accessed December 27, 2017. http://www.kentuckymonthly.com/culture/history/black-patch-tobacco-war/.

16. Soodalter, "Terror in the Night."

17. Day, Jacque. "Western Kentucky's Night Riders: Activists, or Terrorists?" WKMS. Accessed December 27, 2017. http://wkms.org/post/western-kentuckys-night-riders-activists-or-terrorists.

18. Foner, Eric. *Reconstruction: America's Unfinished Revolution, 1863-1877*. New York, New York: Harper & Row., 1988. 425-426.

19. Soodalter, "Terror in the Night."

20. Zycher, Benjamin. "Paul Krugman: A broken window equals economic strength." American Enterprise Institute. June 28, 2013. Accessed December 27, 2017. http://www.aei.org/publication/paul-krugman-a-broken-window-equals-economic-strength/.

21. Saloutos, Theodore. "The American Society of Equity in Kentucky: a recent attempt in agrarian reform." *The Journal of Southern History*, 1939.

22. Borio, Gene. "Tobacco History." Tobacco.org. 2001. Accessed December 27, 2017. http://archive.tobacco.org/History/Tobacco_History.html.

23. Saloutos, "The American Society of Equity in Kentucky."

24. Griffin, Mark. *Stand There and Tremble: When the Night Riders Came to Russellville*. Russellville, Kentucky: Pumpkin Bomb Press, 2007.

25. Weiser, Kathy. "American History: Lynchings & Hangings of America." Legends of America. Updated August 2015. Accessed December 27, 2017. https://www.legendsofamerica.com/ah-lynching6.html.

26. Campbell, Tracy. *The Politics of Despair: Power and Resistance in the Tobacco Wars*. Lexington, Kentucky: The University Press of Kentucky, 1993.

27. "Secretary's Books to be Turned over by Night Rider Leader." *Hopkinsville Kentuckian*, April 18, 1908.

28. "Champion Enlists." *Hopkinsville Kentuckian*, April 16, 1908.

29. Soodalter, "Terror in the Night."

Chapter 4
United States v. American Tobacco Co.

Democrats have always claimed to be "the party of the little guy."[1] Minimum wage. Unions. Labor protections. Voting rights. The list continues.

Come every election season, Liberal media pundits remind American voters of this list while smearing the good name of anyone with a Conservative bone in their body. Fortunately, I think Americans see through the ruse. Democrats—not Republicans—stand behind the Trail of Tears that displaced and killed off thousands of indigenous people and the one-two punch of southern slavery and Jim Crow laws. Naturally, Democrats are happy to pin the blame elsewhere. Revisionist history is a Liberal's best friend.

So it shouldn't come as any surprise that, while Democrats today claim to be the enemies of Big Business, they were *not* the ones to bring down the entrepreneurship-stifling Trusts. While

UNITED STATES V. AMERICAN TOBACCO CO.

"Bernie Bros" today support the economically illiterate Senator Bernie Sanders, many populists of the late nineteenth century fell in love with future President Theodore Roosevelt, a Progressive Republican.[2]

Trust-busting Teddy believed that a lack of economic opportunities was one of the great evils of his day. While the tycoons of industry dined on the finest cuts of meat off fine china, the disenfranchised poor subsisted in third world-like misery. Any good person is horrified at the thought of a homeless five year-old running barefoot through dingy city allies to catch a rat as raw supper, but empathy in and of itself isn't a solution.

The problem I have with the Trusts—Buck Duke's in particular—is the fact that they were the greatest enemies of capitalism. Without a free market, you cannot have *freedom* itself. Men like Duke weren't satisfied with a piece of the profit pie, they wanted the entire pie.

Although I'm not a fan of the Progressive label Teddy Roosevelt was happy to wear, I'm damn proud to be part of the GOP when I read President Roosevelt's words from his 1901 State of the Union speech.

As with John Moody's book *The Truth About the Trusts*, turn of the century language was far more eloquent and precise than today's Common Core vocabulary. To make the excerpts from Roosevelt's speech easy reading, I'll "translate" each paragraph.

TOBACCO, TRUSTS, AND TRUMP

> The mechanism of modern business is so delicate that extreme care must be taken not to interfere with it in a spirit of rashness or ignorance. Many of those who have made it their vocation to denounce the great industrial combinations which are popularly...known as "trusts," appeal especially to hatred and fear... In facing new industrial conditions, the whole history of the world shows that legislation will generally be both unwise and ineffective unless undertaken after calm inquiry and with sober self-restraint.[3]

Teddy's point is that emotion-driven solutions have never been a good idea, especially when they require government intervention.

> There is a widespread conviction in the minds of the American people that the great corporations known as trusts are...hurtful to the general welfare. This springs from no spirit of envy or uncharitableness, nor lack of pride in the great industrial achievements that have placed this country at

UNITED STATES V. AMERICAN TOBACCO CO.

> the head of the nations struggling for commercial supremacy...It is based upon sincere conviction that combination and concentration should be, not prohibited, but supervised and within reasonable limits controlled; and in my judgment this conviction is right.[4]

Rather than an open call for the kind of job-killing regulations that Democrats scream, cry, and beg for today, Roosevelt understood that government's role in business is to be an impartial Referee, not Robin Hood.

> It should be as much the aim of those who seek for social betterment to rid the business world of crimes of cunning as to rid the entire body politic of crimes of violence. Great corporations exist only because they are created and safeguarded by our institutions; and it is therefore our right and our duty to see that they work in harmony with these institutions.[5]

Rules that allow risk-taking small business owners to enter into the market are a terrific idea.

TOBACCO, TRUSTS, AND TRUMP

> When all is said and done, the rule of brotherhood remains as the indispensable prerequisite to success in the kind of national life for which we strive. Each man must work for himself, and unless he so works no outside help can avail him...To be permanently effective, aid must always take the form of helping a man to help himself; and we can all best help ourselves by joining together in the work that is of common interest to all.[6]

Simply put, Teddy believed in Capitalism's power to help the common man and woman lift themselves and their families out of poverty. Because of that, the government is obligated to protect the sanctity of the free market. Even as a Progressive, Roosevelt believed in pulling yourself up by your bootstraps, not expecting others to do it for you. How ashamed he would be of the Welfare State built and maintained by so-called Progressives today!

I'm giving this history lesson to provide a backdrop for the final months of the Tobacco Wars. By the end of President Roosevelt's administration, his Justice Department had broken up forty-four different Trusts, including the largest railroad monopoly in America.[7,8] By 1907, Buck Duke's American

UNITED STATES V. AMERICAN TOBACCO CO.

Tobacco Company found itself in legal trouble as well. The Night Riders' domestic terrorism hadn't gone unnoticed, and neither did their motivation for boycotting the Tobacco Trust. Thanks to vertical consolidation, it was clear to any casual observer that no small business could hope to plant its flag in the tobacco industry. From farms to factories, entrepreneurship was effectively killed off.

Without competition, capitalism cannot work. That's why the "punishment" levied by the feds was to turn a single company into several companies, which could then compete with each other to create a healthier economy.

What President Roosevelt started, his predecessor would finish—another Republican, President William Howard Taft. Buck Duke's lawyers couldn't argue their way out of Taft's Justice Department antitrust lawsuit. The Night Riding incidents that destroyed both life and livelihood raised a red flag so high that no watchdog could ignore it. The humble tobacco farmer got their revenge when, on May 15, 1911, the United States Supreme Court ruled that Buck Duke's American Tobacco Company was in violation of the ultimate antitrust legislation, the 1890 Sherman Antitrust Act.[9]

The reasoning behind the Court's decision was practically right out of a Conservative-leaning textbook. The vertical consolidation business model was deemed a threat to "individual liberty and the public wellbeing," as Chief Justice Edward Douglass White put it.[10]

The federal government wasn't about to stop with Buck Duke's Trust. That same day in 1911, the high court ruled against John D. Rockefeller's Standard Oil.[11] Another monopoly in violation of the Antitrust Act.

The goal of the Sherman Antitrust Act wasn't to punish hard work or success, of course. In Rockefeller's case, dissolution of the Oil Trust into several new companies—Exxon, Mobil, etc.—ended up nearly doubling his wealth![12,13] Rockefeller's peer Buck Duke fared similarly well. *Won't let me have one tobacco company? Fine. I'll own several!*

After the Supreme Court's decision, the one-business Tobacco Trust became the American Tobacco Company, R. J. Reynolds, Liggett and Myers, and Lorillard.[14] Monopolies became oligopolies. Not good, but certainly better. In fact, that was the original intent of the 1890 Sherman Antitrust Act—not to create a perfect marketplace, but to incrementally improve the one that already existed. The 1993 Supreme Court case *Spectrum Sports, Inc. v. McQuillan* gives us a modern English explanation of why the Act needed to be on the books in the first place.

> The law directs itself not against conduct which is competitive...but

UNITED STATES V. AMERICAN TOBACCO CO.

> against conduct which unfairly tends to destroy competition itself.[15]

Again, the government is the Referee, not Robin Hood. Compare that statement to what Massachusetts Senator George Frisbie Hoar had to say, a co-author of Ohio Senator John Sherman's Antitrust Act.

> [A] man who merely by superior skill and intelligence...got the whole business because nobody could do it as well as he could was not a monopolist...[But he was if] it involved something like the use of means which made it impossible for other persons to engage in fair competition.[16]

Clearly, the government's role in the economy is not to directly control or centrally plan anything, it's to protect the market itself. To save capitalism, we had to sacrifice the Trusts. But it was Conservative Republicans, not Liberal Democrats, who were responsible for re-introducing competition into the marketplace.

Unfortunately, like Big Government Liberals now, Big Government advocates circa 1900 didn't respect its boundaries. The Referee wanted to become Robin Hood.

Notes:

1. Allott, Daniel. "Democrats: The party of the little guy no more." *The Washington Examiner*. November 14, 2016. Accessed December 27, 2017. http://www.washingtonexaminer.com/democrats-the-party-of-the-little-guy-no-more/article/2607381.

2. "Teddy Roosevelt and Progressivism." PBS. 2016. Accessed December 27, 2017. http://www.pbs.org/tpt/slavery-by-another-name/themes/progressivism/.

3. Roosevelt, Theodore. "1901 State of the Union Message." The Almanac of Theodore Roosevelt. Accessed December 27, 2017. http://www.theodore-roosevelt.com/images/research/speeches/sotu1.pdf.

4. Roosevelt, "1901 State of the Union Message."

5. Roosevelt, "1901 State of the Union Message."

6. Roosevelt, "1901 State of the Union Message."

7. Schweikart, Larry, Ph.D, and Lynne Pierson Doti, Ph.D. *American Entrepreneur: The Fascinating Stories of the People Who Defined Business in the United States*. New York, New York: AMACOM, 2009.

8. Ruddy, Daniel. *Theodore the Great: Conservative Crusader*. Washington, DC: Regnery History, 2016.

9. Brandt, Allan M. *The Cigarette Century: The Rise, Fall, and Deadly Persistence of the Product that Defined America*. New York, New York: Basic Books, 2007. 39-41.

10. United States v. American Tobacco Co., 221 U.S. 106 (1911). https://supreme.justia.com/cases/federal/us/221/106/case.html

11. Brandt, *The Cigarette Century*.

12. Standard Oil Co. of New Jersey v. United States, 221 U.S. 1 (1910). https://supreme.justia.com/cases/federal/us/221/1/case.html

13. Segall, Grant. *John D. Rockefeller: Anointed With Oil*. Oxford: Oxford University Press, 2001. 93, 112.

14. Brandt, *The Cigarette Century*.

15. Rogers, C. Paul, III, Stephen Calkins, Mark R. Patterson, and William R. Andersen. *Antitrust Law: Policy and Practice*. Newark, New Jersey: LexisNexis, 2008.

16. Adler, Edward A. "Monopolizing at Common Law and under Section Two of the Sherman Act." *Harvard Law Review* 31, no. 2 (December 1917): 246-70. Accessed December 27, 2017. doi:10.2307/1327529.

Chapter 5
When Government "Helps"

When are government solutions the answer to economic problems? A textbook Libertarian answer would probably be, "Never!" but in a country of over three hundred million people, simple answers are not easy solutions. That's why I take a practical approach to government involvement in the days of the Night Riders and today in the age of Trump.

So far, we've explored the rise of the tobacco farming industry after the Civil War, the Duke Trust that sent tobacco prices through a hole in the basement floor, and the intervention of the Feds to police turn-of-the-century monopolies. If this were a war—and it was to the Night Riders—there would be three different armies: the workers, the businesses, and the federal government.

Anyone leaning Left would think that working class people were natural allies of the federal gov-

WHEN GOVERNMENT "HELPS"

ernment in opposition to the so-called Robber Barons. But history tells a different story than Establishment talking points. It usually does.

In the last chapter, I showed how principled Conservatives responded to the economic challenges of a hundred-plus years ago. But not everyone believes in the rights of the individual like Teddy Roosevelt did. That's why my exposé of the antitrust movement makes even more sense when you know *why* Big Government has a vested interest in the success of the One Percent. While today's Occupy Wall Street protesters and their Establishment sponsors think free markets are the root of all evil, they have no idea that Uncle Sam and the Monopoly Man have always been shameless lovers behind closed doors.

While Dr. Amoss' Night Riders did their thing all over Kentucky, Tennessee, and the Carolinas in 1907, Buck Duke kept most of his attention on a series of events that had the potential to ruin his fortune more than any boycott. As depicted in John Moody's Trust chart, the relationships between and among the fortunes of John D. Rockefeller and J.P. Morgan, the banks of New York, and industry Trusts like the American Tobacco Company formed one giant web. What affected one Trust affected everyone. That's another reason Duke and Rockefeller lost their Supreme Court cases on the same day in 1911.

TOBACCO, TRUSTS, AND TRUMP

Four years earlier, another Trust was about to bite the dust—but not at the gavel-wielding hand of Trust-Busting Teddy's administration.

Live by vertical consolidation, die by vertical consolidation.

Two German-Irish brothers, mining experts, and partners in literal crime, F. Augustus and Otto Heinze, saw the makings of an incredible deal in the copper business. While the Amalgamated Copper Mining Company of Butte, Montana, dominated the copper industry, the Heinze brothers, particularly F. Augustus, knew the potential wealth a single Trust could amass.[1,2]

Borrowing Rockefeller's monopolization tactics, F. Augustus leveraged over eighty million dollars of capital to consolidate several smaller companies into one.[3,4] The Montana Ore Purchasing Company, Nipper Consolidated Copper Company, Minnie Healy Mining Company, Corra Rock-Island Mining Company, and Belmont Mining Company became the United Copper Company—a true Trust.[5]

Like Buck Duke had done with the American Tobacco Company, the Heinze brothers got in on the action of the New York Stock Exchange. And like Buck Duke, the Heinze brothers let greed guide them to shoot for the number one spot in their own industry.

With the support of infamous Wall Street fraudster and World War I profiteer Charles W. Morse, the Heinze brothers made their move to "corner

WHEN GOVERNMENT "HELPS"

the market."[6,7] The idea was simple. Otto would splurge on United Copper Company stock, sending the price per share so high that St. Peter could see it up at the Pearly Gates. Majority ownership for the brothers, achieved. Then, he would come calling on Wall Street speculators who hoped to make a quick buck if the United Copper stock price ever dropped.

These speculators had a scheme of their own, one which included five steps: borrow United Copper stock, sell it at the current price, wait for the price to drop, repurchase shares at a lower price to replace the borrowed ones, and pocket the difference.

The Heinze boys planned to beat these short-sellers at their own game. Gobbling up shares of stock would have the opposite effect the speculators hoped, they assumed. With the new share price higher, Otto would demand that the speculators pay for their borrowed shares at the new, higher price.

To kick off the plan, F. Augustus and Otto tried to strike a deal with the third-largest Trust in New York City, one of the largest banks in all of America, the Knickerbocker Trust Company. This was the same bank that funded Charles W. Morse when he cornered the ice market to whet his own appetite for wealth.

But the bank turned the brothers down. Against Morse's advice, on Monday October 14th, Otto Heinze charged ahead with Plan B, dumping whatever pocket change he could scrape together into

TOBACCO, TRUSTS, AND TRUMP

United Copper stock. By the next day, the per-share stock price had nearly doubled. Then, Otto demanded that the short-sellers return their borrowed stock, and he waited for those suckers to crawl on all fours to meet his demands.

Only one problem—he and F. Augustus didn't own the majority of shares needed to make the scheme work. A skyscraper-sized oversight. Without enough funding to purchase enough stock, no one took Otto's threat seriously; the speculators could borrow from other investors.

Only Plan A could have worked for the Henize brothers. By Wednesday afternoon, United Copper traded for ten bucks a share, down from nearly sixty the previous day. That's what happens when the stock market is spooked.

A day later, Otto was banned from the New York Stock Exchange. His brokerage house Otto and Kleeberg went bankrupt. F. Augustus had his own consequences to face. The bank he owned—the State Savings Bank of Butte—and the bank for which he served as president—the Mercantile National Bank of New York City—were both...how can I put this...*screwed*.

A spark of greed grew to a wildfire of fear by week's end. News of the Heinze brothers' conspiracy moved like a deadly virus from bank depositor to depositor all over Manhattan. By the hundreds, people stormed any bank associated with the Heinze brothers to withdraw their money—a classic "bank

WHEN GOVERNMENT "HELPS"

run." Both F. Augustus and mentor Charles Morse received lifetime bans from banking.

The flames of the Heinze family forest fire spread to other properties over the next few weeks. Even though the Knickerbocker Trust Company refused to play Otto's market cornering game, the bank's president Charles T. Barney found himself without a job. Knickerbocker bank runs had left the board with no choice but to claim some good PR by scapegoating Barney. His association with the Heinze brothers remained his only crime. Disgraced for life, he shot himself in the gut with a revolver.[8,9] A slow, tortuous suicide felt more just than an instant, painless one, I suppose.

Then, Knickerbocker itself joined Barney in the grave after J.P. Morgan's National Bank of Commerce refused to (literally) lend a helping hand.[10] In a scene straight out of *It's a Wonderful Life*, families across America rushed their own banks and huddled like sardines around the teller windows.

Where deposits were affected, so were loans. What bank in its right mind would offer a loan in this kind of market? To offset risk, interest rates reached an unprecedented seventy percent for stock brokers on the New York Stock Exchange seeking loans to buy stock. With panic gripping anyone with a bank account, it was up to Big Business and Big Government to do something...anything. J.P. Morgan and the United States Treasury agreed to pump both private and public money into financial institutions to solve the bank run problem. John D. Rockefeller and over a dozen other bank presidents soon joined them, bringing the total of pledged funds into the tens of millions of dollars.[11,12]

Like every scheme documented in this chapter so far, this one failed, too. Even with new money flowing, bankers were as thrilled about offering loans as a fisherman casting a line without bait.

As with most public disasters, the knee-jerk reaction of Americans is to throw more money at the problem—a hundred million dollars to be exact, this bundle put up by the New York Clearing House.[13]

Since only the Trusts and the banks funding them were affected directly by the Heinze brothers, the crisis didn't become a depression. But a crisis is still a crisis. Over the following year, national unemployment rose by eight percent while production fell by eleven percent and imports by twenty-six percent.[14]

Whatever games the One Percent were playing, weren't working for the average American. They still don't work today—see Chapter 7 for more on that. Now you can see why the Populists of the 1900's stood opposed to the Trusts! Not only did monopolization pull the rug out from under small businesses, it threatened the entire finance industry.

What frustrates me most about the Panic of 1907 is not the evaporating wealth of the millionaires and

WHEN GOVERNMENT "HELPS"

billionaires of Wall Street, but the fact that they ran right into the arms of the federal government, which happily wiped their tears and kissed their bruises.

In response to this crisis, the Referee then went behind America's back to get only *one* team's opinion on rewriting the rules—in that team's favor. That team was not the American people.

No matter how sorely our feelings are hurt by the unholy alliance between Big Government and the One Percent, we've got to align ourselves with the facts. Just because the fat cats take the handouts without a second thought doesn't mean hardworking American citizens should. There are *always* strings attached to federal giveaways, and the little guy doesn't have a pair of scissors.

Back in the 1970's, two percent of Americans were on food stamps. Today, that number has reached fifteen percent—a sevenfold increase in just four decades.[15] In some states, people can earn more money by living off taxpayer dollars than you do from an actual career! And overall, entitlement spending is a hundred times higher than fifty years ago.[16]

I'm convinced there's a better way. Whether you're a janitor at a public library or a serial entrepreneur with a net worth in the millions, what would it look like if you didn't accept handouts and instead opted for hand-ups?

How would government policy work if we followed President Teddy Roosevelt's belief that "aid must always take the form of helping a man to help himself?"[17]

Government assistance is a slippery slope. A little help in 1907 from the United States Treasury to keep the big banks afloat—and the Trusts that relied upon them—has given way to a bloated entitlement budget today. There is still a place for truly Progressive policies that make life better for the little guy *not* at the expense of businesses, and vice-versa. The tobacco industry is a case study of federal aid that works. But it was aid that "took the form of helping a man to help himself."

To prevent the financial ruin of tobacco farmers that lead to the Tobacco Wars, the federal government instituted a Tobacco Price Support Program to keep prices stable starting in 1938. The government purchased surplus product from farmers, then sold it for a profit when the market price rose.[18] The program set a quota limiting how much tobacco a single farmer could grow. In keeping with fiscal Conservative ideals, starting in 1982, the program was required to operate at a net cost of zero to taxpayers.[19] Rather than robbing from the rich to give to the poor, this program helped the poor help themselves. There is a place for aid—as long as it subsidizes work ethic, not laziness.

As another example, the father of the cash register industry, John H. Patterson of Dayton, Ohio, was what we today might call "a compassionate Conservative." The free market isn't freedom from a conscience, after all.

WHEN GOVERNMENT "HELPS"

Because his factories sat in the wretched parts of town, Patterson witnessed firsthand the plight of the working poor and their unemployed family and friends. Instead of turning up his nose, he reached out to help the least of these...to help themselves.

He owned a plot of land close to the National Cash Register campus. To put it to use as a "Boys' Garden," he hired a local gardener to teach the inner city kids how to plant, raise, and harvest staple crops. After putting that nutritious food on the table for their working parents and younger siblings, the boys-turned-businessmen sold the remaining harvest at market. The profit went to books and clothes for school.[20]

"Helping a man to help himself."

The facts of history proved Teddy Roosevelt right. If only that was good enough for the Democratic party. The facts of human nature, on the other hand, proved that the Left's accountability-free platform is a much easier sell.

"The rich are out to get you! You can't make it on your own! Your employer takes advantage of you! You're a victim! Fight for fifteen! Social justice!"

The same bill of goods that many Americans buy today was first sold to us in the aftermath of the Tobacco Wars. What a shame we bought it.

Notes:

1. "The United Copper Company Incorporated." *The New York Times*, April 29, 1902. Accessed December 27, 2017. http://query.nytimes.com/mem/archive-free/pdf?res=9C04E5D6103BE733A2575AC2A9629C946397D6CF.

2. Bruner, Robert F., and Sean D. Carr. *The Panic of 1907: Lessons Learned from the Market's Perfect Storm*. Hoboken, New Jersey: John Wiley & Sons, 2007.

3. "Heinze's New Company." *Anaconda Standard*, June 7, 1901.

4. "Heinze forms a Syndicate." *Anaconda Standard*, April 27, 1902.

5. "The United Copper Company Incorporated." *The New York Times*.

6. Bruner, et al. *The Panic of 1907*.

7. "Corner A Market." Investopedia. Accessed December 27, 2017. https://www.investopedia.com/terms/c/corneramarket.asp.

8. "C.T. Barney Dies, a Suicide. Ex-President of the Knickerbocker Trust Co. Shoots Himself in His Home." *The New York Times*, November 15, 1907.

9. Tallman, Ellis W., and Jon R. Moen. "Lessons from the Panic of 1907." *Federal Reserve Bank of Atlanta Economic Review*, May & June 1990. Accessed December 27, 2017. https://www.frbatlanta.org/-/media/documents/filelegacydocs/ern390tallman.pdf.

10. Bruner, et al. *The Panic of 1907*.

11. Tallman, et al. "Lessons from the Panic of 1907."

12. Bruner, et al. *The Panic of 1907*.

13. Tallman, et al. "Lessons from the Panic of 1907."

14. Bruner, et al. *The Panic of 1907*.

15. May, Caroline. "Food stamp use reaches another high in September: 47.7 million participants." The Daily Caller. December 9, 2012. Accessed December 27, 2017. http://dailycaller.com/2012/12/09/food-stamp-use-reaches-another-high-in-september-47-7-million-participants/.

16. Cary, Mary Kate. "The Shocking Truth on Entitlements." U.S. News & World Report. December 19, 2012.

Accessed December 27, 2017. https://www.usnews.com/opinion/articles/2012/12/19/the-shocking-truth-on-entitlements.

17. Roosevelt, Theodore. "1901 State of the Union Message." The Almanac of Theodore Roosevelt. Accessed December 27, 2017. http://www.theodore-roosevelt.com/images/research/speeches/sotu1.pdf.

18. Womach, Jasper. "Tobacco Price Support: An Overview of the Program." *Congressional Research Service*, December 2005. http://research.policyarchive.org/260.pdf.

19. "H.R.6590 - No Net Cost Tobacco Program Act of 1982." Congress.gov. Accessed December 27, 2017. https://www.congress.gov/bill/97th-congress/house-bill/6590.

20. Mattox, A.H. "Boys' Garden School of the National Cash Register Company." Edited by Josiah Strong and William Howe Tolman. *Social Service*, January 1902. Accessed December 27, 2017. https://books.google.com/books?id=pBbLAAAAMAAJ&pg=PA8&lpg=PA8&dq.

Chapter 6
Populists, Socialists, and the Taxes They Love

"If you've got a business—you didn't build that. Somebody else made that happen."[1]

Ex-President Barack Hussein Obama made this remark on July 13th, 2012. In just fourteen words, he encapsulated the ideological shift that first appeared in American politics one hundred years ago.

As you now know, true Progressives—those who believe in progress for all Americans—count good statesmen like President Theodore Roosevelt among their numbers. They believe in the Conservative principle of a strong work ethic and in laws that favor the rights of the individual. But the bigger government has become, the less a single citizen matters in the grand scheme of things. That's why modern-day Leftist Progressives like Obama, the Clintons, and their cronies believe that the have-not's are entitled to the rewards of work done by the

POPULISTS, SOCIALISTS, AND THE TAXES THEY LOVE

have's. And they believe it's their job to make this immoral redistribution happen.

It wasn't always this way. Only a few thousand Americans who were born before income taxes are still alive. This fact begs the question—two questions, actually. Where did income tax come from? And what does it have to do with the Trusts and the men who built them, like Buck Duke and John D. Rockefeller?

No high school or college textbook will tell you this, but the answer to both questions is one in the same. It all starts with the aftermath of the Tobacco Wars and the financial crisis that took place right in the middle of it, the so-called "Panic of 1907."

While the working class got the short end of the stick, the wealthy sought refuge among the Feds to protect their Wall Street fortunes. Unfortunately, President Roosevelt's charge to Americans to lift ourselves out of poverty got replaced by the same idea that Obama based his infamous words on—*the best solution is a government one*.

"Oh, what's that? Bootstrapping entrepreneurs in middle America are doing well on their own? Let's raise their taxes so welfare queens in Democrat-controlled cities can buy that fourth iPad for the seventh kid they had from their fifth baby daddy!"

This is barely an exaggeration of what Lefties like Obama and the Clintons believe. Like you read in the last chapter, policies that hurt the hard-work-

TOBACCO, TRUSTS, AND TRUMP

ing in favor of the hard-leisuring are part of their playbook. Maybe they do have good intentions...is what I would write if I didn't know any better.

The idea that the Trusts and banks of 1900's and 1910's America were "too big to fail" came back to haunt us a hundred years later. We didn't learn our lesson during the Great Recession, and we didn't learn it during the Panic a hundred and ten years ago. If we had, President Woodrow Wilson wouldn't have been able to swing the pendulum of the American people's opinion from a sensible Right-of-center to the far Left. But that's exactly what he did. You see, Wilson prided himself on being a Progressive, but not the type of man Roosevelt was.[2] Wilson believed in a Progressivism that was synonymous with Globalism. This is the idea that decisions should be made at the highest levels of government and business based on how they affect everyone on the planet. The individual be damned![3] That's why he wanted to create the League of Nations after the Great War—the bumbling forerunner to today's global disgrace known as the United Nations. I've always said we need to kick the bums out of their building in New York City and turn the place into luxury housing for disabled Veterans. Maybe someone will listen to me one day.

What allowed Woodrow Wilson to coast into power was his willingness to ride the same wave that would've given Senator Bernie Sanders the

POPULISTS, SOCIALISTS, AND THE TAXES THEY LOVE

2016 Democratic Presidential Nomination if it weren't for Hillary Clinton's shameless puppet, the clown show otherwise known as the Democratic National Committee—populism. Populism is the movement or idea that the needs of the common person matter more than those of the privileged elite.[4] However nice this may sound, there is a good kind of Populism—"Make America great again!"—and a bad kind of Populism—"Make the rich pay their fair share!"

Although not a self-described Populist himself, Wilson tapped into the Left-leaning Populist sentiments of his day, which piggybacked on the Communist idea of "wealth redistribution."[5] Historian Kevin Phillips actually uses this term to describe early twentieth century Democrats' motivation for taxation.

> As both government and the national debt giantized in the twentieth century, the effects of debt had less to do with public spending and broader economic distribution...[T]his Democratic brand of wealth and income redistribution struck hard at certain assets and after-tax incomes...[6]

Just as the Trusts began to (illegally) kill off small business ventures in the 1890's, a third party known

TOBACCO, TRUSTS, AND TRUMP

as the Populist Party of the United States came to prominence. Organized by southern and midwestern farmers, this group looked to the Feds for salvation from economic challenges.[7,8,9] One leader of the Populist Party was quoted as saying, "The fruits of the toil of millions are boldly stolen to build up colossal fortunes for a few."[10] My great-grandfathers found themselves in the middle of violence because that statement was true; the Duke fortune only existed because it was true.

Rather than grab ahold of Teddy Roosevelt's vision for hand-up's, many of my ancestors' peers preferred the idea of handouts. Once the feds abandoned their responsibility as the Referee in the aftermath of the Panic of 1907 (see Chapter 5), it was inevitable that the common man would demand a portion of the bailouts given to the One Percent.

So it shouldn't be a surprise that the idea of a federal income tax—taking from one to give to another—first appeared during the same years that the Night Riders burned barns, fields, and warehouses.[11] The Populists on the Left, all supporters of Woodrow Wilson, embraced this idea. *Those dirty Robber Barons should pay their fair share!*

In other words, income tax came to exist simply because my Great-Grandfather's generation wanted revenge. Can you blame them?

But when you look to the government to solve your problems, expect them to create even more. In

POPULISTS, SOCIALISTS, AND THE TAXES THEY LOVE

order to help balance the federal budget and keep the Robber Barons in check, both of the previous Republican Presidents—Theodore Roosevelt and William Howard Taft—considered the idea of higher taxes, unfortunately.[12]

Once you let Uncle Sam get his fingertips into your pocket, don't be surprised to find his whole fist in there, clinging tightly to everything you've worked hard for. What the Progressive Republicans merely considered, the Populist Democrats made reality.

The public outcry over Trusts run amok—and the Feds' half-assed attempts to protect working Americans from the consequences—brought about a change to our Constitution. Just one month before the Leftist Progressive hero Woodrow Wilson took the Oath of Office, it was official—the 16th Amendment was ratified.

> The Congress shall have Power to lay and collect Taxes, Duties, Imposts and Excises, to pay the Debts and provide for the common Defence and general Welfare of the United States; but all Duties, Imposts and Excises shall be uniform throughout the United States.[13]

It had only taken four years for three-quarters of States to ratify the Amendment, as the Constitution requires. To make the Amendment practical, Congress played their role on the legislative side of things. The anti-tariff, anti-monopoly Revenue Act of 1913 passed both houses before it became law thanks to the Progressive pen of newly inaugurated President Woodrow Wilson.[14]

Just as TEA Party members are ridiculed by the mainstream Liberal media, income tax skeptics were shamed and then ignored before the Revenue Act passed. Despite the overwhelming support from Democrats for this new intrusion into private citizens' pockets, one Democratic Senator, John Sharp Williams of Tennessee, warned his fellow Congressmen about the future of unbridled taxation.

> No honest man can make war upon great fortunes per se. The Democratic Party never has done it; and when the Democratic Party begins to do it, it will cease to be the Democratic Party and become the socialistic party of the United States; or better expressed, the communistic party, or quasi-communistic party, of the United States.[15]

He was right. The 1913 Revenue Act put in place a progressive income tax rate ranging from one percent

POPULISTS, SOCIALISTS, AND THE TAXES THEY LOVE

to seven percent in compliance with the new Constitutional Amendment.[16] Only five years later, a morbidly expensive war motivated by misguided Progressive Globalist principles gave Congress the excuse to do exactly what Senator Williams warned against. The Revenue Act of 1918 took that highest tax rate of seven percent and increased it *elevenfold* to seventy-seven percent.[17] Federal revenue from personal income taxes ended up funding one-third of all expenses for a war that saw three hundred and twenty thousand American casualties...for no good reason.[18,19] I deeply respect and support our troops, but I have neither sentiment—respect or support—for the Progressives who put our brave soldiers' lives at risk to fluff their own Globalist egos.

Before the 1913 bill, Massachusetts Republican Senator Henry Cabot Lodge issued a warning about income taxes—and their consequences—that echoed Senator Williams' eloquent statement. Lodge believed that the Revenue Act was simply "confiscation of property under the guise of taxation."[20]

If only the little guy had taken the two Senators seriously.

If only the little guy had begged both Democrats and Republicans to listen to reason.

If only the little guy had realized that Leftist government solutions come at a steep price.

Today, the descendants of those who protested for an income tax on the rich, are the victims of those hundred year-old pleas for fairness and equity. The average American is now required by law to work 113 days into the year before they get to keep even a *penny* of what their labor is worth.[21] This number is calculated based on how many days Americans as a whole have to work in order to pay our government's tax burden. "Tax Freedom Day" on or around April 23rd every year marks the day that Americans are free to actually receive the compensation they've worked for. Of course, taxes are collected throughout the year, but this day stands as a symbol of shame for us as a nation.

Did you know that Americans collectively spend more on taxes every year than they do on food, clothing, and housing *combined*? And for what? Besides sending soldiers to die fighting overseas in Globalist wars that enrich the military industrial complex, that is.

Leftists sold the dream to America that they could force the rich to pay their fair share. In spectacular fashion, it's backfired. The dream of fairness has become a nightmare of injustice. But thanks to the announcement of unprecedented tax cuts under the Administration of President Donald J. Trump, perhaps the federal government can start to right one of its greatest wrongs.

I'm not saying that the idea of taxes in and of itself is downright evil. We need police and fire services, roads to drive our cars on, and a strong military to defend our freedoms. What I'm opposed to is the "quasi-communistic" obsession that Lefties have with taking from those who work and produce to redistribute it to those who do neither. It sickens me.

Bottom line, what appeared to help working Americans out—taxing the rich—ended up hurting the working class most. What irony.

This, of course, was intentional. Because the people writing the rules were the same ones creating loopholes inside of them. Card-carrying members of the Establishment have escaped the spotlight of truth from shining a blinding light on their deeds... until the next chapter.

Notes:

1. "Obama to business owners: 'You didn't build that'." FOX News. July 16, 2012. Accessed December 27, 2017. http://www.foxnews.com/politics/2012/07/15/obama-dashes-american-dream-suggests-nobody-achieves-success-alone.html.

2. Pestritto, Ronald. "Woodrow Wilson: Godfather of Liberalism." The Heritage Foundation. July 31, 2012. Accessed December 27, 2017. http://www.heritage.org/political-process/report/woodrow-wilson-godfather-liberalism.

3. Gomez, Christian. "Groomed for Globalism." The New American. April 29, 2011. Accessed December 27, 2017. https://www.thenewamerican.com/culture/education/item/288-groomed-for-globalism.

4. "Populism." Business Dictionary. Accessed December 27, 2017. http://www.businessdictionary.com/definition/populism.html.

5. Kengor, Paul G. "The "Purpose" and "Job" of Government: Wealth Redistribution?" The Center for Vision & Values at Grove City College. February 24, 2011. Accessed December 27, 2017. http://www.visionandvalues.org/2011/02/the-purpose-and-job-of-government-wealth-redistribution/.

6. Phillips, Kevin. *Wealth and Democracy: A Political History of the American Rich*. New York, New York: Broadway Books, 2002. 217.

7. Knight, Peter, ed. *Conspiracy Theories in American History: An Encyclopedia*. 2 vols. Santa Barbara, California: ABC-CLIO, 2003.

8. Pollack, Norman. *The Populist Response to Industrial America: Midwestern Populist Thought*. Cambridge, Massachusetts: Harvard University Press, 1976. 11-12.

9. Palmer, Bruce. *Man Over Money: the Southern Populist Critique of American Capitalism*. Chapel Hill, North Carolina: University of North Carolina Press, 1980.

10. "Populist Platform 1892: Preamble." Annenberg Learner. Accessed December 27, 2017. https://www.learner.org/workshops/primarysources/corporations/docs/popplat.html.

11. Young, Adam. "The Origin of the Income Tax." Mises Institute. September 7, 2004. Accessed December 27, 2017. https://mises.org/library/origin-income-tax.

12. "The Income Tax Arrives." Tax History Project. Accessed December 27, 2017. http://www.taxhistory.org/www/website.nsf/Web/THM1901.

13. Fishkin, Joseph R., William E. Forbath, and Erik M. Jensen. "The Sixteenth Amendment." National Constitution Center. Accessed December 27, 2017. https://constitutioncenter.org/interactive-constitution/amendments/amendment-xvi.

14. Koba, Mark. "The Revenue Act Of 1913: 100 Years Of The Income Tax; 73,000 Pages Added Since Wilson Signed Law." FOX Nation. October 4, 2013. Accessed December 27, 2017. http://nation.foxnews.com/2013/10/04/revenue-act-1913-100-years-income-tax-73000-pages-added-wilson-signed-law.

15. Seligman, Edwin R. A. *The Income Tax: A Study of the History, Theory, and Practice of Income Taxation at Home and Abroad*. New York, New York: The Macmillan Company, 1914.

16. Underwood-Simmons Act. ch. 16, 38 Stat. 166 (1913).

17. "History of Federal Income Tax Rates: 1913 – 2017." Bradford Tax Institute. Accessed December 27, 2017. https://bradfordtaxinstitute.com/Free_Resources/Federal-Income-Tax-Rates.aspx.

18. "1917 War Revenue Act passed in U.S." History. Accessed December 27, 2017. http://www.history.com/this-day-in-history/war-revenue-act-passed-in-u-s.

19. Bylerly, Carol R., Ute Daniel, Peter Gatrell, Oliver Janz, Heather Jones, Jennifer Keene, Alan Kramer, and Bill Nasson. "War Losses (USA)." *1914-1918-online. International Encyclopedia of the First World War*. October 8, 2014. Accessed December 27, 2017. doi:10.15463/ie1418.10162.

20. Ratner, Sidney. *Taxation and Democracy in America*. New York, New York: John Wiley and Sons, 1967. 331.

21. Greenberg, Scott. "Tax Freedom Day 2017 is April 23rd." The Tax Foundation. April 18, 2017. Accessed December 27, 2017. https://taxfoundation.org/tax-freedom-day-2017/.

Chapter 7
Filling the Swamp

I don't believe in trickle-down economics. I'm not talking about the slanderous label that Lefties give to entrepreneurship-driven capitalism; I'm talking about the trickle-down model that floated to the top of Americans' minds a hundred years ago: Tax the rich, and let that money trickle down to everyone else.

This effort hasn't worked like Populist Progressive Liberals claimed it would. I might have said "... *believed* it would," but that isn't the truth. On some level, early twentieth century Big Government bureaucrats knew they couldn't keep their promises about equality, fairness, and redistribution.

When you trust the Establishment to write the rules, you can also trust them to *exempt* themselves from those rules. We see that precedent *re*set every time Congress passes a new piece of legislation while making sure their families are protected from the consequences.[1]

FILLING THE SWAMP

"Brand New Congress" (BNC) exists to solve that problem.² I love the idea of firing public employees whose approval rate hovers a sliver above ten percent.³ Unfortunately, BNC has been overrun by Leftists, so I'll instead refer you to the rallying cry of the 2016 Presidential Election, "Drain the swamp."⁴

The swamp has been around for awhile. What happened in the decade after the Tobacco Wars made sure that swamp swallowed as much of our economy into its bureaucratic, hypocritical slime as possible.

I'll explain why I use those adjectives—bureaucratic and hypocritical—in a moment. But first, a story...

> Picture a party of the nation's greatest bankers stealing out of New York on a private railroad car under cover of darkness, stealthily riding hundreds of miles South, embarking on a mysterious launch, sneaking onto an island deserted by all but a few servants, living there a full week under such rigid secrecy that the names of not one of them was once mentioned, lest the servants learn the identity and disclose to the world this strangest, most secret expedition in the history of American finance.⁵

TOBACCO, TRUSTS, AND TRUMP

These words are not my own; they're an account of the night of November 22nd, 1910, penned by *Forbes* magazine founder Bertie Charles Forbes.

After the Panic of 1907, Trust-builders like Buck Duke and his Manhattan high society banking friends got a little antsy about the future of their fortunes. For good reason; the Referee known as the federal government hadn't done a good job about protecting the competitive framework of capitalism before President Teddy Roosevelt (or after, for that matter).

When pro-Big Government influencers want a solution to a problem we face in America, what do they do? They look to the socialist governments of Europe. Today, Leftists scream, cry, plead, and beg for higher taxes to support a universal healthcare system similar to what self-bankrupting Europe has today.[6] I have a timeshare condo in South Beach to sell anyone who believes universal healthcare is a good idea.

The proponents of Big Government did the same thing a hundred years ago. Instead of healthcare, their primary concern was banking. At that time, the United States had no central bank.[7]

Following the Panic, a pair of Republican congressmen, Representative Edward Vreeland of New York and Senator Nelson Aldrich of Rhode Island, put together a bill that was intended to repurpose "the best" of Europe's central banking system for the United States.[8,9] Without the support of a single Democrat, Aldrich and Vreeland rounded up the

FILLING THE SWAMP

Republican support they needed for their Aldrich-Vreeland Currency Law before its passage in 1908.[10] Sure, the law was fairly tame. It allowed banks to issue emergency currency in the event of bank runs to prevent a repeat of the Panic one year prior.[11] The legislation also resulted in the formation of the National Monetary Commission (NMC), which Senator Aldrich led as its Chairman.[12]

It might surprise you that I support the mission of Aldrich's commission! In theory, the NMC was to be a new Referee in the world of American finance, preventing any single political or business interest from taking the economy hostage like the Heinze brothers had nearly done in 1907. But the winds of Populist change blew Aldrich and company in a different direction over the next two years, a direction which had lasting negative consequences for every American taxpayer today.

On that private island on the humid night of November 22nd, 1910, Senator Nelson Aldrich himself stepped out of that railroad car.[13] Beside him stood Abram Piatt Andrew, Jr., a decorated war veteran and Assistant Secretary of the United States Treasury Department.[14,15,16]

They weren't alone. Their fellow passengers included Paul Warburg, Partner at investment bank Kuhn, Loeb and Company and direct descendant of the del-Banco family, the 16th century Jewish bankers whose loans helped build Venice; Frank

Vanderlip, President of New York's National City Bank, former Assistant Treasury Secretary, and California real estate tycoon; and Henry Pomeroy Davison, Benjamin Strong, and Charles Norton, all affiliates of J.P. Morgan.[17,18,19,20,21] Senator Aldrich himself was officially allied with John D. Rockefeller, whose son John D., Jr. married Aldrich's daughter.

Together, this handful of men represented *one-quarter* of the wealth on planet Earth.[22] Their purpose, simply put, was to change the world forever—Big Business and Big Government aligned.

To quote more of Forbes' account of the under-cover-of-darkness meeting, Senator Aldrich planned "...to keep them locked up at Jekyll Island, out of the rest of the world, until they had evolved and compiled a scientific currency system for the United States, the real birth of the present Federal Reserve System, the plan done on Jekyll Island."[23]

What's so special about Jekyll Island, Georgia? Why choose that as the site to brainstorm the Federal Reserve?

For one, its members included the families of Henry Hyde, founder of the largest life insurance company in the world at the time; Marshall Field, Chicago's department store serial entrepreneur; Joseph Pulitzer, the creator of Yellow Journalism, otherwise known as the original "Fake News"; and Wil-

FILLING THE SWAMP

liam Vanderbilt of the Vanderbilt railroad Trust.[24] All of the million-dollar mansions, luxury suites, and seaside summer cottages of Jekyll Island happen to be built on a swamp.

That's right. The undisclosed conference that permanently altered the American economy was held *in a swamp*. This couldn't be better if I made it all up.

The reason why I'm happy to paint such a negative portrait of the 1910 Jekyll Island meetings is the fact that they led directly to the creation of the Federal Reserve which, of course, was signed into law by the Patriarch of the Left, President Woodrow Wilson.

On December 23rd, 1913, the Federal Reserve Act enacted permanent changes to our banking system.

> An Act to provide for the establishment of Federal reserve banks, to furnish an elastic currency, to afford means of rediscounting commercial paper, to establish a more effective supervision of banking in the United States, and for other purposes.[25]

To some, this might look like a wild conspiracy theory that blames every economic depression, retraction, and recession on the Establishment. Isn't *some* regulation a good thing? Didn't the banking system need *some* sort of government oversight?

I'd be happy to answer those questions, but we have to remember, the Federal Government is like a bad date who asks you out for a friendly drink and expects to be in bed with you before midnight. It only took five years for a tiny tax on the rich to skyrocket to seventy-seven percent, after all.[26]

So while I'll leave the textbook analyses up to the qualified and credentialed Economists over at The Heritage Foundation, my job is to show what happened when that first domino of federal intrusion into banking fell.

Coupled with the new progressive income tax, it was only a matter of time before the Federal Reserve wielded more control over individuals' lives than Founding Father Alexander Hamilton could have possibly imagined—one of America's first proponents of central banking.[27]

Make no bones about it, the Federal Reserve is a modern-day banking cartel that hardly anyone knows anything about.[28] Any sane American should support Senator Rand Paul's "Audit the Fed" idea for that very reason.[29] With the way things are going, maybe that will actually happen someday. The sooner the better.

In the same way that the Revenue Act of 1913 ultimately led to the creation of the Internal Revenue Service—and their unbridled appetite for the ripe fruits of hard-working Americans' labor—the Jekyll Island-conceived Federal Reserve Act can be blamed for the Great Recession.

In January 2011, the bipartisan U.S. Financial Crisis Inquiry Commission released the official list of causes for the Great Recession. One of the first guilty parties listed in the report is the Federal Reserve itself and its inability to deal with the toxic mortgages that homeowners all over America defaulted on from 2007 through 2009.[30]

Those toxic mortgages, of course, were the result of the Democrats' pet project known as the Community Reinvestment Act, which encouraged working class families—minorities in particular—to get loans for homes they otherwise couldn't have afforded. The Feds tilted the rules in favor of one team, and everybody lost as a result.[31,32]

Thanks to the Community Reinvestment Act, private financial institutions were required to lower their lending standards. Combine that with the Federal Reserve's control over mortgage interest rates, and you have the makings of unmitigated disaster.

That's exactly what we got ten years ago. While the Federal Reserve was busy bailing out banks because they were "too big to fail"—just as the Treasury had done a hundred years prior—middle class America got the short end of the stick.[33] Have we learned nothing about government intervention in the last hundred years?

At this point, I could get into supply-side economic theory or nominal gross domestic product, but again, I'm not an economist. I am, however, aware of the patterns of history that repeat themselves right before our eyes.

Before researching this book, I knew there had to be some sort of connection between Buck Duke, the Night Riders, and the Tobacco Trust, and the invisible hand of the Establishment dealing cards that benefitted themselves at the expense of individual Americans. I did not expect to find what I did.

Clearly, it is not unreasonable to say that the Big Government-Big Business relationship that formed a hundred-plus years ago—a relationship that gave birth to the Internal Revenue Service and the Federal Reserve—has left more economic devastation on the average American than any other "enemies, foreign and domestic."

And we know what the Constitution says Congress' power is to deal with such enemies. Rather than get off on that tangent, I want to make clear why the good ole One Percenters were complicit in this unknown war against individual rights.

While Big Government spokespeople were happy to praise higher taxes while Trusts decimated small business—just as they are today—they ensured that taxation laws protected their fortunes. Populist demagogues benefitted from the message of taxing the rich via income taxes then, over time, ensuring that their corporations remained protect-

FILLING THE SWAMP

ed inside the lesser-taxed walls of legal loopholes.[34]

In other words, Leftists have pushed those income taxes higher and higher to seemingly "punish" those evil Robber Barons like Buck Duke. But all the while, they keep friends in the federal government who do their best to protect their business' incomes.

Scratch my back, I'll scratch yours.

The result has been a wicked cycle of corporate donors placing politicians in office who enshrine policies favorable to their corporations to keep that money a-flowin'. That's why I shook my head when a *Rolling Stone* article started off their character assassination of Mitt Romney a few months before the 2012 Presidential Election with this line:

> How does a private-equity kingpin worth at least $250 million pay a lower tax rate – just 14 percent – than many teachers and firemen?[35]

Of course, when One Percenters like Hillary Clinton flaunt their fortunes, the Left shuts the hell up. They're happy to shield themselves from the effects of "fairness" and "equality" to keep their corporate donor friends well-fed.[36,37]

That's why I agree with President Donald J. Trump in his encouragement of Hillary Clinton to run against him a second time in 2020![38] And while she's at it, why not have a conversation about all of those private speeches she gave to her Wall Street friends behind closed doors?[39]

Scratch my back, I'll scratch yours.

The hypocrisy is obvious now, and it was obvious during the Tobacco Wars, the Panic of 1907, and the Populist movement that put tax-lover Woodrow Wilson into the Oval Office. When Statist One Percenters like Warren Buffet praise the benefits of socialism, it's time to get skeptical. Meanwhile, he's probably shelling out millions of dollars to tax accountants to protect a hell of a lot of wealth within tax code loopholes.[40]

Of course, the Liberal mainstream media has little to say about him because sizeable portions of his wealth end up funding Democrats' campaigns.[41]

Fortunately, I do see the tide turning. Since Barack Hussein Obama occupied the White House in 2008, Americans have turned cities, counties, and state houses Republican-red from sea to shining sea.[42] In the process, he practically bankrupted the Democratic National Committee.[43] Thanks, Obama!

However, the story of entrepreneurship-killing Big Business and individual rights-annihilating Big Government didn't end in the 1910's. We're still dealing with the dominoes of destruction that have fallen since our representatives made choices to give Uncle Sam an increasingly short leash to "fix" our problems.

When you want the Referee to become Robin Hood, you're not going to like the results.

FILLING THE SWAMP

Before, during, and after the Tobacco Wars era, Robin Hood committed his fair share of crimes—against the people who expected him to help.

The Declaration of Independence declares that Life, Liberty, and the Pursuit of Happiness are inalienable rights that belong to everyone.[44] But when the Establishment sees the glitter of gold, expect them to do whatever it takes to get their sweaty, swampy hands all over it...even if it means the result is *death*.

The Tobacco Wars were not the only instance of Americans killing one another for the sake of a meager profit. Many lives have been stolen, liberties seized, and happiness taken.

All because the One Percent got greedy.

Notes:

1. "Congress exempt from several federal laws." FOX News. February 3, 2012. Accessed December 27, 2017. http://www.foxnews.com/us/2012/02/03/congress-exempt-from-several-federal-laws.html.

2. Guttenplan, D.D. "Is Brand New Congress the Future of Progressive Politics?" *The Nation*. August 11, 2016. Accessed December 30, 2017. https://www.thenation.com/article/is-brand-new-congress-the-future-of-progressive-politics/.

3. "Congress and the Public." Gallup News. Accessed December 27, 2017. http://news.gallup.com/poll/1600/congress-public.aspx.

4. McKelway, Doug. "The First 100 Days: Can Trump really 'drain the swamp'?" FOX News. December 9, 2016. Accessed December 30, 2017. http://www.foxnews.com/politics/2016/12/09/first-100-days-can-trump-really-drain-swamp.html.

5. Griffin, G. Edward. *The Creature from Jekyll Island: A Second Look at the Federal Reserve*. Westlake Village, California: American Media, 1994.

6. Varney, Stuart. "The left wants America to be more like Europe: Varney." FOX Business. October 19, 2017. Accessed December 27, 2017. http://www.foxbusiness.com/politics/2017/10/19/left-wants-america-to-be-more-like-europe-varney.html.

7. Prins, Nomi. *All the Presidents' Bankers: The Hidden Alliances that Drive American Power*. New York, New York: Nation Books, 2014.

8. Miron, Jeffrey A. "Financial Panics, the Seasonality of the Nominal Interest Rate, and the Founding of the Fed." *The American Economic Review* 76, no. 1 (March 1986): 125-140. https://fraser.stlouisfed.org/files/docs/publications/aer/aer_1986_miron_financial_panics.pdf.

9. Whitehouse, Michael A. "Paul Warburg's Crusade to Establish a Central Bank in the United States." *The Region*, May 1, 1989. Accessed December 27, 2017. https://www.minneapolisfed.org/publications/the-region/paul-warburgs-crusade-to-establish-a-central-bank-in-the-united-states.

10. "New currency bill passes the House." *The New York Times*, May 28, 1908.

11. Wells, Donald. *The Federal Reserve System: A History*. Jefferson, North Carolina: McFarland, 2004.

12. Dewald, William G. "The national monetary commission: a look back." *Journal of Money, Credit and Banking* 4, no. 4 (November 1972): 930-56. doi:10.2307/1991235.

13. Richardson, Gary, and Jessie Romero. "The Meeting at Jekyll Island." Federal Reserve History. December 4, 2015. Accessed December 27, 2017. https://www.federalreservehistory.org/essays/jekyll_island_conference.

14. *The National Cyclopaedia of American Biography*. Supplement 1. New York, New York: James T. White and Company, 1910.

15. "Abram Piatt Andrew." Hall of Valor/Military Times. Accessed December 27, 2017. http://valor.militarytimes.com/recipient.php?recipientid=17195.

16. Sleeper, Henry Davis. *Beauport Chronicle: The Intimate Letters of Henry Davis Sleeper to Abram Piatt Andrew, Jr., 1906-1915*. Gloucester, Massachusetts: Society for the Preservation of New England Antiquities, 1991.

17. Birmingham, Stephen. *Our Crowd: The Great Jewish Families of New York*. Syracuse, New York: Syracuse University Press, 1996. 190.

18. „Frank Vanderlip, Banker, Dies At 72. Former Head of National City Had Served as Assistant Secretary of Treasury." *The New York Times*, June 30, 1937.

19. Griffin, *The Creature from Jekyll Island.*

20. Bagwell, Tyler E. "The Jekyll Island duck hunt that created the Federal Reserve." Jekyll Island History. Accessed December 27, 2017. http://www.jekyllislandhistory.com/federalreserve.shtml.

21. Garraty, John A., and Jerome L. Sternstein, eds. *Encyclopedia of American Biography*. New York, New York: Harper & Row, 1974. 25-27.

22. Griffin, G. Edward. "A Talk by G. Edward Griffin: *Author of The Creature from Jekyll Island*." Bigeye. Accessed December 30, 2017. http://www.bigeye.com/griffin.htm.

23. Snyder, Michael. "The Federal Reserve Is Holding A Conference On Jekyll Island To Celebrate 100 Years Of Dominating America." Business Insider. November 3, 2010. Accessed December 27, 2017. http://www.businessinsider.com/fed-jekyll-island-club-2010-11.

24. Hunter, John. "Jekyll Island." New Georgia Encyclopedia. July 17, 2003. Accessed December 27, 2017. http://www.georgiaencyclopedia.org/articles/geography-environment/jekyll-island.

25. "Federal Reserve Act." Board of Governors of the Federal Reserve System. Accessed December 27, 2017. https://www.federalreserve.gov/aboutthefed/fract.htm.

26. "Historical Highlights of the IRS." Internal Revenue Service. Accessed December 27, 2017. https://www.irs.gov/newsroom/historical-highlights-of-the-irs.

27. DiLorenzo, Thomas J. "The Corrupt Origins of Central Banking." Mises Institute. December 2008. Accessed December 27, 2017. https://mises.org/library/corrupt-origins-central-banking.

28. Henderson, Dean. "The Federal Reserve Cartel: The Eight Families." Global Research. June 1, 2011. Accessed December 27, 2017. https://www.globalresearch.ca/the-federal-reserve-cartel-the-eight-families/25080.

29. Freeman, Brian. "Sen. Paul: Time to Defy Critics and Pass 'Audit the Fed' Act." Newsmax. August 21, 2017. Accessed December 30, 2017. https://www.newsmax.com/newsfront/rand-paul-audit-the-fed-act-establishment-central-bank/2017/08/21/id/808831/.

30. Yeebo, Yepoka. "Financial Crisis Inquiry Commission's 10 Major Findings." The Huffington Post. January 27, 2011. Accessed December 27, 2017. https://www.huffingtonpost.com/2011/01/27/financial-crisis-inquiry-commission-findings_n_814935.html.

31. Bhutta, Neil, and Daniel Ringo. "Assessing the Community Reinvestment Act's Role in the Financial Crisis." Board of Governors of the Federal Reserve System. May 26, 2015. Accessed December 27, 2017. https://www.federalreserve.gov/econresdata/notes/feds-notes/2015/assessing-the-community-reinvestment-acts-role-in-the-financial-crisis-20150526.html.

32. "Community Reinvestment Act." Federal Financial Institutions Examination Council. Accessed December 27, 2017. https://www.ffiec.gov/cra/default.htm.

33. "Too Big To Fail." Investopedia. Accessed December 27, 2017. https://www.investopedia.com/terms/t/too-big-to-fail.asp.

34. Kiyosaki, Robert T., and Sharon L. Lechter. *Rich Dad Poor Dad: What the Rich Teach Their Kids About Money That the Poor and Middle Class Do Not!* New York, New York: Grand Central Publishing, 2000.

35. Dickinson, Tim. "Mitt Romney's Tax Dodge." *Rolling Stone*, October 25, 2012. October 12, 2012. Accessed December 27, 2017. https://www.rollingstone.com/politics/news/mitt-romney-s-tax-dodge-20121012.

36. Simon, Ellen. "Hillary Clinton's Wall Street Ties." Investopedia. Accessed December 27, 2017. https://www.investopedia.com/articles/investing/030415/hillary-clintons-wall-street-ties.asp.

37. "Wall Street for Hillary?: Clinton has $48.5M in hedge fund backing, compared to Trump's $19K." FOX News. July 30, 2016. Accessed December 27, 2017. http://www.foxnews.com/politics/2016/07/30/wall-street-for-hillary-clinton-has-48-5m-in-hedge-fund-backing-compared-to-trumps-19m.html.

38. Hayes, Christal. "Trump Wants to Run in 2020 Election Against the Woman He Already Beat: Hillary Clinton." Newsweek. October 16, 2017. Accessed December 27, 2017. http://www.newsweek.com/trump-wants-run-2020-election-against-woman-he-already-beat-hillary-clinton-685743.

39. "Top adviser on Clinton Wall Street speeches: 'It's pretty bad.'" FOX News. October 24, 2016. Accessed December 27, 2017. http://www.foxnews.com/politics/2016/10/24/top-adviser-on-clinton-wall-street-speeches-its-pretty-bad.html.

40. Elkins, Kathleen. "Bernie Sanders made more than $1 million last year—here's how much it takes to be in the top 1%." CNBC. June 7, 2017. Accessed December 27, 2017. https://www.cnbc.com/2017/06/06/bernie-sanders-made-over-1-million-last-year-and-has-joined-the-1-percent.html.

41. Debenedetti, Gabriel. "Bernie begins raising cash for down-ballot progressives." Politico. April 13, 2016. Accessed December 27, 2017. https://www.politico.com/story/2016/04/bernie-sanders-progressives-fundraising-221887.

42. Malone, Clare. "Barack Obama Won The White House, But Democrats Lost The Country." FiveThirtyEight. January 19, 2017. Accessed December 27, 2017. https://fivethirtyeight.com/features/barack-obama-won-the-white-house-but-democrats-lost-the-country/.

43. Boyer, Dave. "Brazile says she found DNC deep in debt from Obama, controlled by Clinton a year before nomination." *The Washington Times*. November 2, 2017. Accessed December 27, 2017. https://www.washingtontimes.com/news/2017/nov/2/brazile-says-obama-left-dnc-deep-debt-clinton-camp/.

44. Jacobs, James. "The Meaning of "Life, Liberty, and the Pursuit of Happiness"." *Crisis Magazine*. July 4, 2017. Accessed December 30, 2017. http://www.crisismagazine.com/2017/life-liberty-pursuit-happiness.

Chapter 8
When the Little Guy Stands Up for Himself

Near the headquarters of my company—Rumford Industrial Group—there is a factory that builds robots to replace people. From heavy industrial operations to manual labor on assembly lines, these robots threaten the thousands of jobs that (still) remain in the blue collar sector of North America.

I don't want to demonize this business, of course. The future rides on the rails of technology, after all. I do believe you can be a legitimate Progressive without sacrificing economic freedom or individual sovereignty, which happened throughout the early twentieth century as the have's clashed with the have-not's.

Every time I drive by that factory on the way to my office, I think about those clashes. Every revolution that upsets the status quo leaves somebody unhappy. The appearance of vertical consolidation ultimately led to the Tobacco Wars, after all.

WHEN THE LITTLE GUY STANDS UP FOR HIMSELF

But other workers had it much, *much* worse than the Bracken County tobacco farmer. He only lost his farm. Other working class people, from railroad workers to coal miners, faced the one-two punch of Big Business and Big Government allied against them...and lost their lives.

Two years before Washington Duke set up shop in the tobacco manufacturing business, a battle of David against Goliath shook the railroad industry from coast to coast. Most Americans have never heard of the First Great Depression, which began in 1873 when bumbling bankers in New York City triggered bank runs that should have been called bank *rampages*.[1,2]

The man who had just funded the Union war effort, Jay Cooke of investment bank Jay Cooke and Company, went bankrupt attempting to make a fortune off the construction of the Northern Pacific Railway.[3] Bank after bank failed immediately after, which affected states as far away as Nevada and California.[4,5] Workers took to the streets to protest, only to get beaten up by police. Sound familiar?

The railroads felt the shockwave of Depression the worst—particularly the workers. After the Civil War, an onslaught of poor immigrants competing for blue collar jobs had increased competition, which lowered wages.[6] The casual attitudes of Robber Barons towards the working conditions of employees—many of them under eighteen—further angered the people. By the time 1877 rolled around, railroad workers had plenty of reasons to be mad as hell. On July 14th, the employees of the Baltimore & Ohio Railroad had enough. In Martinsburg, West Virginia, workers went on strike. Only after their third pay cut that year had been rescinded, they would get back to work.[7,8]

When state militia troops refused to fire upon the striking workers to teach them a lesson, this one localized protest spread to Albany, Baltimore, Buffalo, Chicago, Philadelphia, Pittsburgh, Scranton, St. Louis, and Syracuse.[9,10,11,12,13,14] Railroad employees and coal miners of all ages dropped their tools, left the job sites, and refused to lift a finger until working conditions changed and wages rose. To numb what was otherwise a growing pain of the free market, President Rutherford B. Hayes sent federal troops to throw some water on the protestors' fiery rage.[15]

If only the Referee allowed the economy to work itself out, business owners would have made life better for their employees because of the profit motive. No entrepreneur wants workers who hate their guts! But once again, the Referee didn't do his job.

Dozens of protesters were shot and killed.[16] Apparently needing to take care of your family is a

WHEN THE LITTLE GUY STANDS UP FOR HIMSELF

death sentence when the State gets involved. During the riots in Reading, Pennsylvania, workers marched, burned, demonstrated, and picketed.[17] You would have thought it was Berkley before a Conservative speaker showed up!

In response, the powers-that-be employed the private army known as the Pinkerton National Detective Agency. These mercenaries joined the state militia in the shameless massacre of civilian strikers.

To exacerbate the workers' plight, Judge Thomas Drummond of the 7th Circuit Court of Appeals ruled that, "A strike or other unlawful interference with the trains will be a violation of the United States law, and the court will be bound to take notice of it and enforce the penalty."[18]

It was official; Team Big Government joined Team Big Business. If you protested because your employer expected you to work for nearly free in an environment about as clean as a sewer and as safe as a dynamite factory, you were a *criminal*.

This sequence of events—Big Business hurts the people, the people protest, Big Government comes to Big Business' rescue—happened over and over during post-Industrial Revolution America. Just four years prior to the railroad strikes, the Irish mafia—"Molly Maguires"—led a coal mining strike in Pennsylvania which disintegrated into a revolt.[19,20] The bodies of both murdered miners and managers were found, sparking the kind of hate-filled finger-pointing that America wouldn't see again until the Democrats fumbled the 2016 Presidential Election right into Donald J. Trump's lap. The President of the Philadelphia and Reading Railroad, Franklin Gowen, hired the cigar-chomping thugs at the Pinkerton National Detective Agency to end the chaos as violently as necessary.[21]

Thanks to the testimony of obviously biased Pinkerton agents, nearly two dozen strikers were arrested and several were executed without the due process of law.[22] Former Carbon County judge John Lavelle wrote about this miscarriage of justice over one hundred and twenty years later:

> The Molly Maguire trials were a surrender of state sovereignty. A private corporation initiated the investigation through a private detective agency. A private police force arrested the alleged defenders, and private attorneys for the coal companies prosecuted them. The state provided only the courtroom and the gallows.[23]

The alliance of wage-suppressing Big Business and justice-denying Big Government resulted in the deaths—state-sanctioned murders, really—of

WHEN THE LITTLE GUY STANDS UP FOR HIMSELF

hundreds and hundreds of working class people in the years that followed.

From the shooting of seven protesting tradespeople by national guardsmen in Wisconsin in 1886, to the massacre of dozens of black sugar cane workers by federal soldiers and county sheriffs in Louisiana in 1887 and 1888; from the slaughter of more than thirty striking railroad workers in Chicago in 1894, to nineteen Eastern European immigrant coal miners shot by the county sheriff during a peaceful protest in Pennsylvania in 1897; from the four hundred and forty casualties of the 1905 Chicago garment manufacturing riots at the hands of police, to the infamous "Battle of Blair Mountain" in 1920 that left up to one hundred West Virginia coal miners dead, the lesson from history is pretty damn clear.[24,25,26,27,28,29,30,31]

When the little guy stands up for himself, he gets crushed.

Of course, Democrats soon realized that if they pretended to be the guardians of the working class, they could count on their votes—never mind that their policies actually *hurt* the little guy. Remember, business-friendly Republicans want both small and large businesses to treat employees fairly so they can thrive on the job and be promoted. The GOP also believes in slashing taxes so these businesses can create even more career opportunities.[32]

TOBACCO, TRUSTS, AND TRUMP

Looking back on the bloodshed of the individual versus the Establishment, I fear that we are careening toward a labor war that would make the Pinkerton thugs look like Santa Claus. The Trusts grabbed America's workers by the balls through monopolization—lower cost of production, lower cost of goods for the customer, lower wages for the employee.

In many ways, that phenomenon has reemerged. Everyday, that robot factory reminds me that our economy is creeping closer and closer to crisis—if we let it. Already, we've seen millions of blue collar jobs disappear since automation and manual labor outsourcing to other countries came onto the scene, and these trends are going to continue.[33,34] But what's going to happen when the most common job of white men in America—truck driver—vanishes when self-driving vehicles take over? What's going to happen when accountants, tax professionals, paralegals, underwriters, adjusters, loan officers, and cashiers find their careers on the double-axed chopping block of automation and artificial intelligence (AI)?

When an AI software program can read a person's emotions better than another human can—and respond with uncanny empathy—Isaac Asimov's *iRobot* can be considered a documentary, not fiction.[35]

I couldn't help but shake my head when I saw those Occupy Wall Street protesters waving the

WHEN THE LITTLE GUY STANDS UP FOR HIMSELF

"Fight for $15" signs around.[36] Do they want to lose their jobs faster than technology makes them obsolete? After all, if you raise the wages of two seven-fifty an hour hour employees to fifteen dollars an hour, one of them is out of a job.

If we as a society don't open our eyes and look toward the horizon of change, we're going to see twenty-first century Night Riders burning banks, mortgage offices, law firms, and fast food chains because a machine can do our jobs one thousand times better for one-thousandth of the cost.

Instead of complaining when your job vanishes, prepare yourself and your family. Don't Occupy Wall Street, occupy a profitable profession that *benefits* from automation. AI expert J. P. Gownder predicts that by 2027, we will be "working side by side with robots."[37] In certain industries, we've already started to see this happen. International consulting firm Deloitte reviewed the effect of automation technologies on the British technology sector. While eight hundred thousand low-skilled, low-wage jobs were eliminated, over three and a half million higher-skilled, higher-paying jobs were created. On average, those positions paid roughly thirteen thousand dollars more per year and resulted in a net boost of nearly one hundred and eighty-five billion dollars to the United Kingdom economy.[38]

Clearly, the best way our society can respond

TOBACCO, TRUSTS, AND TRUMP

to what might otherwise be devastating changes—eight hundred thousand people lost their jobs in the Deloitte case study, after all—is to rely on the free market. Conservatism 101.

An entrepreneur in the modern, technology-driven steel industry, Drew Greenblatt, has gotten creative about growing his business and retaining employees without denying present and future trends.

> All of a sudden [employees are] super productive and it's because we've given them the tools—it's robotics and automation...Thank God for robots. If it wasn't for robots, these guys would be unemployed.[39]

When you give people the means to help themselves, they will. That's how everyone wins in a changing economy. That was true after the Tobacco Wars and the Panic of 1907, and it's true today. For example, it makes economic sense to pay your employees better. Costco Wholesale employees earn thousands more per year than their uninsured, unhappy counterparts at Wal-Mart.[40] Why do you think Costco is drowning in profits every quarter while Sam's China-to-America Emporium sits on a profit margin so thin it could slice their rusty metal shopping carts right in half?[41,42]

Greenblatt and Costco are in good company, of

WHEN THE LITTLE GUY STANDS UP FOR HIMSELF

course. It was Henry Ford who, in 1914, practically created the middle class out of thin air when he doubled factory wages to five dollars a day—about $120 in today's currency.[43]

When you take care of your employees, they take care of your business; when you take care of your citizens, they take care of the country. The Establishment doesn't get this. I can only hope the rest of America does...before it's too late.

Notes:

1. Furstenberg, Francois. "What history teaches us about the welfare state." *The Washington Post*, July 1, 2011. Accessed December 27, 2017. https://www.washingtonpost.com/opinions/what-history-teaches-us-about-the-welfare-state/2011/07/01/AGGfhFuH_story.html?utm_term=.923b7b68ded5&wprss=rss_opinions.

2. "Financial Panic of 1873." U.S. Department of the Treasury. Accessed December 27, 2017. https://www.treasury.gov/about/education/Pages/Financial-Panic-of-1873.aspx.

3. Lubetkin, M. John. *Jay Cooke's Gamble: The Northern Pacific Railroad, the Sioux, and the Panic of 1873*. Norman, Oklahoma: University of Oklahoma Press, 2006.

4. Loomis, Noel M. *Wells Fargo: An Illustrated History*. New York, New York: Clarkson N. Potter, 1968. 119-120.

5. Masur, Gerhard. *Imperial Berlin*. New York, New York: Basic Books, 1970. 65.

6. Hall, Prescott F. *Immigration and Its Effects Upon the United States*. New York, New York: Henry Holt and Company, 1906.

7. Flank, Lenny. "The 1877 "Great Strike" and the Reading Massacre." Daily Kos. June 5, 2014. Accessed December 27, 2017. https://www.dailykos.com/stories/2014/6/5/1283319/-The-1877-Great-Strike-and-the-Reading-Massacre.

8. Stowell, David O. "Albany's Great Strike of 1877." *New York History* 76, no. 1 (January 1995): 31-55. Accessed December 27, 2017. http://www.jstor.org/stable/23182536?item_view=read_online.

9. Barry, Bill. "New historic marker commemorates the 1877 Railroad Strike at Camden Station." Baltimore Heritage. March 5, 2013. Accessed December 27, 2017. https://baltimoreheritage.org/education/new-historic-marker-commemorates-the-1877-railroad-strike-at-camden-station/.

10. Stowell, David O. *Streets, Railroads, and the Great Strike of 1877*. Chicago, Illinois: The University of Chicago Press, 1999.

11. Adamczyk, Joseph. "Great Railroad Strike of 1877." Encyclopædia Britannica. Accessed December 27, 2017. https://www.britannica.com/topic/Great-Railroad-Strike-of-1877.

12. Hitchcock, Frederick L. *History of Scranton and Its People*. Vol. 1. New York, New York: Lewis Historical Publishing Company, 1914. 496-516.

13. Foner, Philip S. *The Great Labor Uprising of 1877*. Atlanta, Georgia: Pathfinder Press, 1977.

14. Schneirov, Richard. *Labor and Urban Politics: Class Conflict and the Origins of Modern Liberalism in Chicago, 1864-97*. Working Class in American History. Champaign, Illinois: University of Illinois Press, 1998.

15. Salvatore, Nick. "Railroad Workers and the Great Strike of 1877: The View from a Small Midwest City." *Labor History* 21, no. 4 (Fall 1980): 522-545.

16. Adamczyk, "Great Railroad Strike of 1877."

17. Singer, Merrill. *Drugging the Poor: Legal and Illegal Drugs and Social Inequality*. Long Grove, Illinois: Waveland Press, 2007. 47–48.

18. Cahan, Richard. *A Court That Shaped America: Chicago's Federal District Court from Abe Lincoln to Abbie Hoffman*. Evanston, Illinois: Northwestern University Press, 2002. 33-34.

19. McCabe, James Dabney. *The History of the Great Riots*. Philadelphia, Pennsylvania: National Publishing Company, 1877.

20. Loy, Matt. "The Legend of the Molly Maguires." Pennsylvania Center for the Book. Spring 2009. Accessed

December 27, 2017. http://pabook2.libraries.psu.edu/palitmap/Mollies.html.

21. Boyer, Richard O., and Herbert M. Morais. *Labor's Untold Story: The Adventure Story of the Battles, Betrayals and Victories of American Working Men and Women*. 3rd ed. Pittsburgh, Pennsylvania: United Electrical, Radio & Machine Workers of America, 1979.

22. Loy, "The Legend of the Molly Maguires."

23. Lavelle, John P. *The Hard Coal Docket: 150 Years of the Bench & Bar of Carbon County (1843 - 1993)*. Times News, 1984.

24. Nesbit, Robert C. *Urbanization & Industrialization, 1873-1893*. Edited by William Fletcher Thompson. Vol. 3. The History of Wisconsin. Madison, Wisconsin: Wisconsin Historical Society Press, 1985.

25. Hogue, James K. *Uncivil War: Five New Orleans Street Battles and the Rise and Fall of Radical Reconstruction*. Reprint Edition. Baton Rouge, Louisiana: Louisiana State University Press, 2011.

26. Anderson, John W. *Transitions: From Eastern Europe to Anthracite Community to College Classroom*. Bloomington, Indiana: iUniverse, 2005.

27. Miller, Randall M., and William Pencak. *Pennsylvania: A History of the Commonwealth*. State College, Pennsylvania: Penn State Press, 2003

28. Fitch, Robert. *Solidarity for Sale: How Corruption Destroyed the Labor Movement and Undermined America's Promise*. New York, New York: PublicAffairs, 2006.

29. Witwer, David. *Corruption and Reform in the Teamsters Union*. Working Class in American History. Champaign, Illinois: University of Illinois Press, 2003.

30. "History of Great Teamsters' Strike Filled with Sensational Incidents." *Chicago Daily Tribune*. July 21, 1905.

31. Patel, Samir S. "Mountaintop Rescue." *Archaeology* 65, no. 1 (January/February 2012).

32. Gleckman, Howard. "What the GOP Platform Says About Taxes." Tax Policy Center. July 19, 2016. Accessed December 27, 2017. http://www.taxpolicycenter.org/taxvox/what-gop-platform-says-about-taxes.

33. Rotman, David. "How Technology Is Destroying Jobs." MIT Technology Review. June 12, 2013. Accessed

December 27, 2017. https://www.technologyreview.com/s/515926/how-technology-is-destroying-jobs/.

34. Davidson, Paul. "Automation could kill 73 million U.S. jobs by 2030." *USA Today*, November 28, 2017. Accessed December 27, 2017. https://www.usatoday.com/story/money/2017/11/29/automation-could-kill-73-million-u-s-jobs-2030/899878001/.

35. Collins, Katie. "In 1964 Isaac Asimov accurately predicted how technology would look in 2014." *Wired*. January 3, 2014. Accessed December 30, 2017. http://www.wired.co.uk/article/asimov-2014-technology-predictions.

36. Levitin, Michael. "The Triumph of Occupy Wall Street." *The Atlantic*. June 20, 2015. Accessed December 30, 2017. https://www.theatlantic.com/politics/archive/2015/06/the-triumph-of-occupy-wall-street/395408/.

37. Gownder, J. P., Laura Koetzle, Cliff Condon, Kyle McNabb, Christopher Voce, Andrew Bartels, Michele Goetz, Andy Hoar, Clare Garberg, and Diane Lynch. "The Future Of Jobs, 2027: Working Side By Side With Robots." Forrester Research, April 3, 2017. https://www.forrester.com/report/The Future Of Jobs 2027 Working Side By Side With Robots/-/E-RES119861.

38. Insall, Jemma, and Ankur Borthakur. "From Brawn to Brains: The Impact of Technology on Jobs in the UK." Deloitte. 2015. Accessed December 27, 2017. https://www2.deloitte.com/content/dam/Deloitte/uk/Documents/Growth/deloitte-uk-insights-from-brawns-to-brain.pdf.

39. Ghafourifar, Alston. "Automation replaced 800,000 workers... then created 3.5 million new jobs." VentureBeat. September 7, 2017. Accessed December 27, 2017. https://venturebeat.com/2017/09/07/automation-replaced-800000-workers-then-created-3-5-million-new-jobs/.

40. Cascio, Wayne F. "The High Cost of Low Wages." *Harvard Business Review*, December 2006. Accessed December 27, 2017. https://hbr.org/2006/12/the-high-cost-of-low-wages.

41. Sozzi, Brian. "How Costco Is Winning Its Battle Against Wal-Mart's Sam's Club." TheStreet. May 28, 2015. Accessed December 27, 2017. https://www.thestreet.com/story/13166984/1/how-costco-is-winning-its-battle-against-wal-marts-sams-club.html.

42. Bose, Nandita. "Wal-Mart's profit margins fall; quarterly outlook disappoints." Reuters. August 17, 2017. Accessed December 27, 2017. https://www.reuters.com/article/us-walmart-results/wal-marts-profit-margins-fall-quarterly-outlook-disappoints-idUSKCN1AX172.

43. "The Middle Class Took Off 100 Years Ago ... Thanks To Henry Ford?" NPR. January 27, 2014. Accessed December 27, 2017. https://www.npr.org/2014/01/27/267145552/the-middle-class-took-off-100-years-ago-thanks-to-henry-ford.

Chapter 9
The Ultimate Anti-Establishment Career Path

Sales is in my blood. My Dad James "Buster" Rumford, Sr. was a salesman. When he and Mom got married, he raised tobacco to sell and built his own creamery to process and sell milk in Bracken County. Once kids came along, he got a job as a bread man for the Butter Nut Bread Company in Cincinnati.

When I was barely taller than a crop of corn in July, I joined him in the business of sales. All over the west end of Cincinnati, we sold bread and made deliveries to businesses. This was a summer job for me, of course. We did have school back in those days!

I also helped out at my grandparents' farm in Kentucky raising tobacco, baling hay, and milking cows. It sounds tedious, and it sure as hell wasn't a picnic, but seeing the rewards of my own labor firsthand through farmland entrepreneurship taught me the value of hard work. It also taught me how to sell. You might say I was my Dad's secret sales weapon on the job!

THE ULTIMATE ANTI-ESTABLISHMENT CAREER PATH

I share this with you because the slow, deliberate chipping away of the working class in this country by the Establishment has made the self-discipline and self-starting ambition of my youth a thing of the past. Now, kids feel like they're entitled to a living wage even though they can't communicate at a fifth grade level. Minimum talent, minimum wage. Like the workers joked in the Soviet Union, "As long as they pretend to pay us, we'll pretend to work!"[1]

What happened to us? When did America's backbone shatter? Somewhere between the State-sanctioned murder of workers and the burning of tobacco barns by angry farmers, an idea entered into American consciousness and took root: Life should be fair.

It's a tempting thought. But when you take from the have's who earned a reward and give to the have-not's who slacked off all day, you have a society that's anything but just. Tobacco farmers saw their source of cash money run dry thanks to scheming Buck Duke. Today, we're seeing the modern working class whittle away as manual labor jobs get replaced by technology or get exported to other countries.

But there's one career path that has stood the test of time, and I wish more Americans recognized it. That's why I'm devoting this chapter to it—sales-driven entrepreneurship. Given that about one-third of all Americans are working class, the intended audience for this chapter is one hundred million people, give or take.[2]

TOBACCO, TRUSTS, AND TRUMP

It's the fundamental fact of economics that where there are buyers, there are sellers. And where there are consumers, there are producers. Everything else is just the icing on the commerce cake. Rather than waiting for Uncle Sam to reach out a hand promising free stuff—only to smack the American people upside the head with more taxes and fewer freedoms—we've got to take the sales profession seriously.

If only Americans do today what the working class has not done in the past—make your own way, rely on no one else, and seize whatever opportunities you can to depend on the fruit of your own labor. This also means we've got to rediscover work ethic.

Building a business isn't easy. Neither is sales. I would know—I've done both. The good news is, neither requires a college degree, which I do not have. As you know from my own stories, you don't even have to be an adult.

In 1955, my parents moved the family up to Dayton—"Little Detroit," as it was known thanks to the automotive manufacturers' direct connection to General Motors and Chrysler.[3]

To help support myself and the family I took a commission sales job—the definition of entrepreneurship. Every morning, my supervisor loaded me up with ice cream into my pedal cart freezer. From ten to four six days a week, I peddled that thing around town. At the end of every day, I gave my boss his share of the profit and kept mine.

THE ULTIMATE ANTI-ESTABLISHMENT CAREER PATH

Because my income was determined by my performance—the ultimate form of self-reliance—I had no choice but to try my best. How many kids do you know who give it their all at their very first jobs? Probably not many.

Over two summers riding the ice cream pedal cart, I earned one thousand six hundred dollars in commissions. When you taste the fruit of your own labor, you're hooked. During the school year, I traded bicycle pedals for front porch door bells. Going door to door in Dayton's very first suburban neighborhoods, I sold the *Saturday Evening Post*, Bibles, bread, water softeners, then milk. After mastering business-to-customer sales (B2C), I knew I could swim with the big fish where the big money was—business-to-business sales (B2B).

The week I wrote this chapter, I received a plaque from the American Welding Society, commemorating fifty years of my membership. Welding is how I got my start in B2B sales. After a couple of brief stints working as an usher and assistant manager at Dayton's old Lowes Theatre—and mastering the fundamentals of customer service—I looked around for a better opportunity.

Thanks to the booming manufacturing industries of southwest Ohio, I tried my luck as a junior salesman for a multinational welding corporation selling products to GM, Ford, Chrysler, Procter & Gamble, and independent machine shops. If you

TOBACCO, TRUSTS, AND TRUMP

were in the industrial market in southwest Ohio, you were my prospect.

Starting in the welding business when I was twenty-one years old, I was trained by very strong entrepreneurial mentors to understand welding and soldering. We demonstrated this to customers, who purchased our products. Our biggest accomplishment was training the welders at GM to bring them up to speed on the new technology.

I rose through the ranks, earning promotions to District Supervisor and then Regional Manager for the company's midwest five state market area. My old friends from middle and high school told me that the place to work was the factory. But my gut told me that pursuing entrepreneurship—the riskier path—was the right one for me.

With a Presidential election coming up in 1980, I felt the winds of change blow through the corporate world as well. The welding corporation, like the 1800's railroad monopolies and Buck Duke's Tobacco Trust, got greedy. Bloated middle management set higher quotas and lowered commissions to fund their useless white collar salaries. I gave the Divisional Manager in Chicago a piece of my mind about it, and it cost me. Even though I had doubled the welding corporation's business every year from 1977 through 1979, the only thanks I got was a demotion to junior salesman.

THE ULTIMATE ANTI-ESTABLISHMENT CAREER PATH

A week later, I hired an attorney to set up a corporation for me. I had no idea what I was going to sell or to whom. All I knew is that full-blown entrepreneurship was my future. An ad headline in *The Wall Street Journal* from an industrial protective coatings and composites company caught my eye.

"Midwest Distributors Needed."

I knew from a decade and a half in welding sales just how in-demand products were that prevented wear and tear on industrial equipment. While the welding corporation clamped down on this salesman's motivation, the coatings and composites company presented an offer to me that was as close to the true definition of entrepreneurial capitalism as I have ever seen. They manufactured their products and sold them to distributors, who sold them to customers—three levels of entrepreneurship. I was sold.

On my way to Garden City, New York, on April 1st to meet with the composites manufacturer's Founder—who I've always called "The Viking" due to his Danish ancestry—I stopped in to see my current employer, headquartered in Flushing. I turned in my letter of resignation. My official end date was April 30th.

When my divisional manager met me the at the Columbus airport after my flight home, he begged me to stay, "You've been with us for years, and now you're leaving us high and dry?"

TOBACCO, TRUSTS, AND TRUMP

Out of loyalty—and with a little bit of guilt mixed in—I extended my remaining period of employment to June 1st. Then to June 30th.

When you take care of your employees, they take care of your business; the opposite is also true.

On my way to sign the contract with the coatings manufacturer and officially launch my new distribution business—Rumford Industrial Group—I took a detour. The President of my soon-to-be ex-employer wanted to see me one final time. I walked into his office to discuss whatever it was he wanted to discuss. He glanced over top of the thick manilla envelope in his hands, got up, and gave me a quick handshake.

"Jim, I think you need to appreciate everything this company has given you over the years," his nauseating speech started off. "The fact is, we want you to come back. And just as importantly, you need this job."

I really didn't like his condescending tone, but I let him finish. "We're prepared to make it worth your while." He opened the envelope that was clearly too small for whatever contents had been jammed inside it.

"This," he shook the envelope in theatrical fashion, "is the last six months worth of back pay. There is also a check to reimburse you for all travel expenses you would have incurred, another check as a bonus for your performance, and a third check as the first installment of your new salary. It's a massive raise, Jim."

THE ULTIMATE ANTI-ESTABLISHMENT CAREER PATH

I didn't say a word. When someone offers you a handout, it always comes at a steep price.

"But, there is one little detail first." The President put the envelope down on his desk. "All of this is yours if you dissolve your company and void any contracts you have made with your new company. Those are my terms."

"And here are mine," I said, turning towards the open door. "Screw me once, shame on you. Screw me twice, shame on me. You've done it three times. It won't happen again."

I walked out before he got in another word. By lunchtime, I was in The Viking's office signing our paperwork. Rumford Industrial Group was born.

Starting my own company was one of the best choices I've made in my entire life, and it's a testament to the power of a work ethic in a free market. Thanks to The Viking, people like me have been able to launch new entrepreneurial ventures (Rumford Industrial Group). And thanks to people like me, I can now create new job opportunities for self-disciplined, self-motivated professionals (outside sales jobs).

The best thing the Federal Government can do is get out of the way of job creators like me and The Viking. This is how we can get the unemployed back to work in this country. And the best place to start is where I did—a commission sales job. In a position like that, you are worth your work ethic.

TOBACCO, TRUSTS, AND TRUMP

If we don't want our economy—and our society—to spiral into chaos when those manual labor working class jobs are gone thanks to automation and AI, we have to teach people to declare independence from the traditional employment model. Nobody owes anyone a job.

Say what you like about Jeff Bezos, but that man is doing capitalism a big favor. Amazon.com is very similar to Rumford Industrial Group in that it's a distribution channel. Amazon doesn't produce most of the products they sell, of course. They come from manufacturers like members of the Alibaba Group, an ecommerce conglomerate.

And just as I create sales jobs, Amazon has designed a system called "Fulfillment By Amazon" (FBA) that allows anyone to start an ecommerce business, sell their products on Amazon's website, and use Amazon's fulfillment centers to pack and ship their products right to the customer.[4]

Creating your own income has been the path to freedom from Big Business oppression and Big Government tyranny in the past, and it is again. As more and more Americans choose to occupy profitable professions—those directly or indirectly related to sales—the better off our civilization is going to be.

Unfortunately, the next two generations of Americans, which now outnumber Baby Boomers, have already started to follow a different path.[5]

THE ULTIMATE ANTI-ESTABLISHMENT CAREER PATH

Nearly half of Millennials favor socialism over capitalism.[6] That's right; Gen Y prefers the economic model at the heart of Communism, which was responsible for slaughtering upwards of one hundred million people in the twentieth century.[7] What the hell is wrong with us?

Our young people have been seduced by the same platitudes that doomed the working class after the Tobacco Wars and the Panic of 1907 to economic subservience and government dependence.

There's only one group of people responsible for it. You won't be surprised who they are.

Notes:

1. Caldwell, Melissa L. *Not by Bread Alone: Social Support in the New Russia*. Berkeley, California: University of California Press, 2004. 48.

2. Morin, Rich, and Seth Motel. "A Third of Americans Now Say They Are in the Lower Classes." Pew Research Center. September 10, 2012. Accessed December 28, 2017. http://www.pewsocialtrends.org/2012/09/10/a-third-of-americans-now-say-they-are-in-the-lower-classes/.

3. Jiang, Hezi. "Fuyao Glass helps 'Little Detroit' regain jobs, pride." China Watch. *The Washington Post*. April 10, 2017. Accessed December 28, 2017. http://chinawatch.washingtonpost.com/2017/04/fuyao-glass-helps-little-detroit-regain-jobspride/.

4. "Fulfillment by Amazon - Benefits." Amazon Services. Accessed December 28, 2017. https://services.amazon.com/fulfillment-by-amazon/benefits.html.

5. "American Generation Fast Facts." CNN. Updated August 27, 2017. Accessed December 28, 2017. http://www.cnn.com/2013/11/06/us/baby-boomer-generation-fast-facts/index.html.

6. Cardona, Nick. "Survey: 1 in 2 millennials would rather live in a socialist or communist country than capitalist one." AOL. November 3, 2017. Accessed December 28, 2017. https://www.aol.com/article/news/2017/11/03/survey-1-in-2-millennials-would-rather-live-in-a-socialist-or-communist-country-than-capitalist-one/23266418/.

7. Courtois, Stéphane, Nicholas Werth, Jean-Louis Panné, Andrzej Paczkowski, Karel Bartošek, and Jean-Louis Margolin. *The Black Book of Communism: Crimes, Terror, Repression.* Edited by Mark Kramer. Translated by Jonathan Murphy. Cambridge, Massachusetts: Harvard University Press, 1999. 92-97, 116-121.

Chapter 10
Domestic Enemies

When there was only one year left in the reign of now ex-President Barack Hussein Obama, Governor Bobby Jindal of Louisiana told the American people the truth.

> This president's trying to turn the American dream into the European nightmare. He's trying to make us more dependent on government... Give Bernie Sanders credit—at least he's honest enough to call himself a socialist. Hillary Clinton, President Obama—they're no better. They're just not honest enough to call themselves socialists.[1]

The self-mutilating Leftist media jeered, sneered, and snickered.

"Bernie is a hero! Just par for the Democratic course!"

TOBACCO, TRUSTS, AND TRUMP

"You racist a-hole! You're just jealous that Obama is president and you're not!"

"If only we could be so lucky! Having eight years of Socialist Bernie Sanders would be paradise!"

One Progressive pundit after the next was heard spouting off these "rebuttals" to Governor Jindal in the weeks after. With their echo chamber preventing them from hearing a single word of critique, the Democratic lapdogs of the media never got around to asking themselves a very important question.

What if Governor Jindal is right?

But why would they take him seriously? An unbiased investigation of the Governor's statements would distract from their BS opinion pieces posing as actual news stories.

"Down with white Christian male privilege! Raise taxes on the rich, then raise them again! All Republicans are racist, especially the black, Latino, Jewish, and Asian Republicans!"

With quality content like that, who needs legitimate journalism? I swear, if CNN, MSNBC, *Salon*, *The Huffington Post*, and all the usual suspects went bankrupt in the next twenty-four hours, no thinking American would notice they were gone. In the meantime, Governor Jindal's statements stand. So does my question: What if he's right?

What if Obama, Hillary, Bernie, and the Lefties really do want to transform America into a Socialist hellhole?

DOMESTIC ENEMIES

To answer these questions, we have to rewind the clock to the turn-of-the-century America when the heartland was left to burn in the wake of the Tobacco Wars and the east coast metropolitan centers of finance and banking were left to suffer following the Panic of 1907. Right wing and Left wing Progressives duked it out during that period of American history—one side fought for individual rights and small business, the other side for federal intervention and work ethic-annihilating taxation.

For awhile, it looked like sensible Conservatives like President Teddy Roosevelt would win, but the Left won that battle with a low blow—the promise of free stuff.[2,3] Free housing, free food, free jobs, free education, free medical care, and free eugenics.

I include eugenics in the list because it was Leftist Progressives who founded the American eugenics movement, which was responsible for the forced sterilization of so-called undesirables, abortion of unwanted babies, racist immigration policies, the widespread belief in "superior" and "inferior" races, and the idea of gas chamber euthanasia.[4,5,6,7,8,9]

Given that young Americans have become so enthralled with the utopian promises of equality and fairness that are the hallmark of Socialism and Communism, it shouldn't be a surprise that it was American Progressives who birthed the ideas that led directly to the Holocaust during World War II.[10]

TOBACCO, TRUSTS, AND TRUMP

You read that right; American Progressives personally funded the German eugenics program in the 1930's where the infamous "Angel of Death" Dr. Josef Mengele worked. With utopian ideas about racial purity and perfect genes, Mengele went on to torture prisoners of Auschwitz in unspeakable ways.[11,12]

It might seem like we're off on a tangent at this point, and the fact is...*we are*. But think of the American eugenics movement as more like a strand inside a web of tyranny and deceit that has halted America's true progress for more than a century. The public needs to know about the shameless racism and sexism of early twentieth century Progressives because they won. Because of good PR.

What good person wants to be against "women's health care?"[13] Of course, moral degenerates during the twentieth century on the Left defined "women's health care" as forcibly sterilizing minorities and fantasizing about ideas that led to the Holocaust. What good person wants to be in favor of *that* version of "women's health care?"

This opposites language is why we are where we are today. To poor and broke tobacco farmers, to bankrupt small business owners, and to unemployed and hungry working class families, Leftist Progressives have promised the world. Decade after decade for over a hundred years now, terms like "economic justice" and "income equality" have justified job-killing regulations and productivity-

DOMESTIC ENEMIES

draining taxes. Nobody comes out on top when either of those are in play—except Uncle Sam. When you play the house, the house always wins.

Take the words "Robber Baron" as another example. You've read that term throughout this book when I've mentioned men like Andrew Carnegie. Make no mistake—many acts committed by the One Percent were downright wrong, which is why upright and principled men like Teddy Roosevelt went after the tycoons of the Trusts. But was everything that the Carnegies, Dukes, and Rockefellers of the world did...*wrong*?

Absolutely not. But Leftist Progressives would have you believe that no matter how hard a business owner works, they "didn't build that," so of course they are not entitled to the fruits of their labor!

In 1889, Andrew Carnegie published *The Gospel of Wealth*. Rather than look to the federal government to end the squalor of the inner cities and bring prosperity to farms all across the heartland, Carnegie made it clear that because the wealthy *earned* their wealth, *they* should be the ones to share their fortunes—of their own free will.[14]

Notice in this excerpt from *The Gospel of Wealth* how Carnegie agrees with Roosevelt's fundamental belief in the value of the individual. Therefore, the greatest works of charity are those that "help a man to help himself," as Teddy put it.

TOBACCO, TRUSTS, AND TRUMP

[Today the] poor enjoy what the rich could not before afford. What were the luxuries have become the necessaries of life. The laborer has now more comforts than the landlord had a few generations ago. The farmer has more luxuries than the landlord had, and is more richly clad and better housed. The landlord has books and pictures rarer, and appointments more artistic, than the King could then obtain...

The Socialist...who seeks to overturn present conditions is to be regarded as attacking the foundation upon which civilization itself rests, for civilization took its start from the day that the capable, industrious workman said to his incompetent and lazy fellow, "If thou dost net sow, thou shalt net reap," and thus ended primitive Communism by separating the drones from the bees. One who studies this subject will soon be brought face to face with the conclusion that upon the sacredness of property civilization itself depends--the right of the laborer to his hundred dollars in the savings bank, and equally the legal right of the millionaire to his millions...

There remains, then, only one mode of using great fortunes...It is founded upon the present most intense individualism...Under its sway we shall have an ideal state, in which the surplus wealth of the few will become, in the best sense the property of the many...administered for the common good, and this wealth, passing through the hands of the few, can be made a much more potent force for the elevation of our race than if it had been distributed in small sums to the people themselves...

This is the problem of Rich and Poor to be solved. The laws of accumulation will be left free; the laws of distribution free. Individualism will continue, but the millionaire will be but a trustee for the poor; intrusted for a season with a great part of the increased wealth of the community..."The man who dies thus rich dies disgraced."[15]

Carnegie himself lived up to his own ideal, donating approximately ninety percent of his wealth—

nearly three hundred and fifty million dollars—to charitable foundations, public libraries, and colleges and universities.[16] He wasn't coerced or forced into giving any of this. He shared his profits with the poor of his own free will. The tax man played no role in the philanthropy that changed millions of lives for the better.

Leftists don't realize that, by and large, people want to do the right thing—even wealthy people. That's why it should sting the conscience of every hardworking American when Leftist pundits make "wealth" synonymous with "greed." In fact, the phrase "the wealthy are greedy" turns up over sixteen million search results on Google! Who do you think is behind the vast majority of this propaganda?

Again, Progressives like to be perceived as being on the side of good, which is how we ended up with one of the highest corporate tax rates in the world until recently—thirty-nine percent.[17] That's almost double the corporate tax rate of the United Kingdom. It makes you wonder if Lefties don't know how jobs are made.

If you look at the modern-day Progressive platform of the Democratic party, everything they stand for implies something that it isn't—equal pay, affordable housing, a bigger social safety net, collective bargaining rights, immigration reform, and so on.[18]

DOMESTIC ENEMIES

These sure sound like happy ideas. But when Democrats get power—and keep it—every citizen within a one hundred mile radius had better get the hell out.

Investors Business Daily published a report about the absolute worst cities in America to live.[19]

Chicago has suffered like a hog bleeding out on the floor of a slaughterhouse. Every year, thousands of people are shot. Hundreds of them die. In a few years, Chicago will mark the one hundredth anniversary of the last Republican mayor winning an election. What a fine mess the dynamic Liberal duo of gun control laws and Obama's ex-Chief of Staff Rahm Emanuel have made of the place.

Detroit hasn't seen a Republican mayor since the Eisenhower administration. Out of every ten residents, four are just making it by living below the federal poverty line. Once a gem of capitalism and the benefits it shares with both the wealthy and the working classes, Detroit is a case study of what welfare queen turned successful businesswoman Star Parker calls "Uncle Sam's Plantation."[20]

According to *Forbes*, St. Louis is the second most dangerous city in the United States.[21] The last time the GOP had a say in how the city was run, I was preschool age. Today, St. Louis is the unofficial capital of Social Justice Warriors (SJW's), who apparently want to set race relations back a hundred and fifty years—but blame their behavior on police officers.

TOBACCO, TRUSTS, AND TRUMP

Then there are the likes of Atlanta, Buffalo, Cleveland, El Paso, Miami, Newark, Oakland, and Philadelphia. The longer Democrats have held power in these cities, the more poverty, crime, gang violence, and drug abuse have held the working class hostage.

So why the hell do voters keep these sorry excuses of leaders in office? Because they've become convinced through manipulative messaging every election that the Lefties have the people's best interests in mind. Clearly they do not. All the Lefties have to do is promise more handouts, and low-income voters show up at the polls looking for any name with the D-word next to it.

Corrupt politicians are basically running a business. They and their Establishment friends *need* voters to keep voting in the best interest of the State, not their own. Why do you think deadly opioids are legal while the plants that attract hippies are not? Because the business needs customers.

Look at how the justice system works, specifically in Democrat-controlled cities. It's literally a business. The salespeople are law enforcement who target everyday people on the street with half a sandwich bag worth of weed. The judges and prosecutors who steal these men from their families for years at a time are the operations administrators. The prisons are inventory warehouses, and the customers who keep this cycle of injustice running smoothly

DOMESTIC ENEMIES

are the taxpayers and voters. The Establishment has this down to a science. Even certain Republicans have wanted to get in on this action over the years, unfortunately.

Overall, history has shown that it is consistently the Democrats who delude the average American into paying for—and voting for—policies that are not in their best interest. Even the Left-leaning *Baltimore Sun* cannot help but comment on this tragedy. In an op-ed the newspaper published before the 2016 Presidential Election, investor Richard Franz told it like it is.

> Many African Americans, sold on the concept that the Democrats represent the little guy, have consistently helped get…Democrats elected. I would ask the black voters of these cities to seriously question whether they believe their lives have been materially improved since their grandparents lived there… [Y]ou will never hear [Democrats] look inward and consider that perhaps their leadership and well-meaning but poorly advised liberal social agendas are to blame for much of the misery in poor urban communities.[22]

TOBACCO, TRUSTS, AND TRUMP

Richard, I'm with you on all but the well-meaning part.

With the facts as clear as the reason President Donald J. Trump deserves a second term (see Chapter 11), why do so many people support Progressives? Why is it that Democrats hold almost two hundred and forty combined House and Senate seats instead of zero?[23,24]

Many schools within our education system—but obviously not all—have fallen into the trap of Left wing propaganda, which teaches students that right is wrong and wrong is right. How else can you explain the fact that kids these days are falling in love with murderous Communism?

Once the Progressive idea of hand-outs not hand-ups reached the mainstream during Woodrow Wilson's era, there was no going back. In the decades that followed, the National Education Association (NEA) made it their mission to indoctrinate America's youth with even more Leftist ideologies.[25,26,27] While our military was poised to defend the homeland from Soviet aggression, kids back home were being taught by their government-approved textbooks that Socialism and Communism are GOOD for working and middle class America!

An ex-Socialist journalist named Verne P. Kaub investigated the Progressive propaganda that weaseled its way into our country's classrooms. He published an exposé entitled *Communist-Socialist*

DOMESTIC ENEMIES

Propaganda in American Schools. Kaub's book should be required reading by every student. I bet the Left would have none of that since it's practically their playbook!

> No technique of the propagandists for Communism-Socialism is more satisfying to its users or more effective in preparing the minds of both adults and young people...than the "debunking" of American history, which includes gross misrepresentation of the character and aims of the Founders and of the historical documents they wrote...Other Communist-Socialist techniques used by the NEA spokesmen include praise of Soviet "accomplishments"...[28]

This is exactly what we see today. We are taught by the Establishment to apologize for our history, take down the statues of good men, and look to Socialist countries for how we should live our lives. After the above excerpt, Kaub warns of a dirty little trick that Progressives still use today to smear and silence anyone who dares call them out.

> [T]o promote the ideology of collectivism, false leaders are willing

TOBACCO, TRUSTS, AND TRUMP

> to stoop to the lowest and slimiest of Communist-Socialist tricks. One of these tricks...is to declare that all anti-Communists must be, *per se*, pro-Fascist.[29]

This is precisely what the Establishment has done to supporters of President Trump. Because, like the President, I don't buy into Socialism or SJW's or "fairness" or hand-outs, people like me are labelled "Alt-Right extremists" and "neo-Fascists." Kaub saw this coming decades ago! They will character-assassinate you at any cost. The recent screams from the Left to do away with the Electoral College are simply echoes of what Soviet sympathizers said a long time ago. Kaub warned about this, too.

> Prominent in this [Progressive] propaganda is...the slogan is..."Democratic control—one member, one vote"...[A]n American citizen who is devoted to the idea of the importance and dignity of the individual [does not] toy with the philosophy of Socialism, which robs the citizen of his most important right to own property and to care for his family from the fruits of his own toil.[30]

DOMESTIC ENEMIES

Governor Jindal was right. Because the Lefties want Socialism—and because they've been lying to working class farmers and laborers about it since my Great-Grandparents' generation—I'd say they fit the description of the "domestic enemies" that our public officials are sworn to protect us from.

Wouldn't you?

Maybe someone will do something about it someday.

Maybe someone already has.

Maybe that someone happens to be the 45th President of the United States.

Notes:

1. Lavender, Paige. "Bobby Jindal Gives Bernie Sanders Some Credit." The Huffington Post. August 3, 2015. Accessed December 28, 2017. https://www.huffingtonpost.com/entry/bobby-jindal-bernie-sanders_us_55bffbede4b06363d5a34398.

2. Knight, Robert. "Obama's Free Stuff Army." *The Washington Times*. January 25, 2015. Accessed December 28, 2017. https://www.washingtontimes.com/news/2015/jan/25/robert-knight-obamas-free-stuff-army/.

3. Thompson, Catherine. "Debate Moderator: How Can You Compete With 'Free Stuff' From Dems?" Talking Points Memo. November 10, 2015. Accessed December 28, 2017. http://talkingpointsmemo.com/livewire/trish-regan-democrats-free-stuff.

4. Stern, Alexandra. *Eugenic Nation: Faults and Frontiers of Better Breeding in Modern America*. Berkeley, California: University of California Press. 27-31.

5. Will, George F. "The liberals who loved eugenics." *The Washington Post*. March 8, 2017. Accessed December 28, 2017. https://www.washingtonpost.com/opinions/the-liberals-who-loved-eugenics/2017/03/08/0cc5e9a0-0362-11e7-b9fa-ed727b644a0b_story.html?utm_term=.f70f29b331f8.

6. Harris, Malcolm. "The Dark History of Liberal Reform." New Republic. January 21, 2016. Accessed December 28, 2017. https://newrepublic.com/article/128144/dark-history-liberal-reform.

7. Kluchin, Rebecca M. *Fit to Be Tied: Sterilization and Reproductive Rights in America 1950–1980*. New Brunswick, New Jersey: Rutgers University Press, 2009. 17-20.

8. Schoen, Johanna. *Choice and Coercion: Birth Control, Sterilization, and Abortion in Public Health and Welfare*. Chapel Hill, North Carolina: University of North Carolina Press, 2005.

9. Black, Edwin. "Eugenics and the Nazis – the California connection." *San Francisco Chronicle*, November 9, 2003.

10. Kühl, Stefan. *The Nazi Connection: Eugenics, American Racism, and German National Socialism*. Paperback ed. Oxford, United Kingdom: Oxford University Press, 2002. 36.

11. Black, "Eugenics and the Nazis – the California connection."

12. Kubica, Helena. *Anatomy of the Auschwitz Death Camp*. Edited by Yisrael Gutman and Michael Berenbaum. Published in association with the United States Holocaust Memorial Museum, Washington, D.C. Bloomington and Indianapolis, Indiana: Indiana University Press, 1994.

13. Cohen, David S., and Carol Sanger. "Jane Doe, Abortion and the Attack on Women's Healthcare Under Trump." U.S. News & World Report. October 30, 2017. Accessed December 28, 2017. https://www.usnews.com/opinion/op-ed/articles/2017-10-30/jane-doe-abortion-and-the-attack-on-womens-health-care-under-trump.

14. Carnegie, Andrew. *The Gospel of Wealth and Other Timely Essays*. New York, New York: The Century Co., 1901. Accessed December 28, 2017. https://books.google.com/books?id=q5ALvRp6lwgC&printsec.

15. Carnegie, The Gospel of Wealth and Other Timely Essays.

16. "Andrew Carnegie's Story." Carnegie Corporation of New York. 2015. Accessed December 28, 2017. https://www.carnegie.org/interactives/foundersstory.

17. Pomerleau, Kyle. "CBO Report Compares U.S. Corporate Tax to G20." Tax Foundation. March 16, 2017. Accessed December 28, 2017. https://taxfoundation.org/cbo-report-compares-us-corporate-tax-g20/.

DOMESTIC ENEMIES

18. Yglesias, Matthew. "Elizabeth Warren's 11 commandments for progressives show Democrats don't disagree on much." Vox. July 21, 2014. Accessed December 28, 2017. https://www.vox.com/2014/7/21/5918063/elizabeth-warrens-11-commandments-for-progressives-show-democrats.

19. "How Decades Of Democratic Rule Ruined Some Of Our Finest Cities." Investor's Business Daily. March 9, 2016. Accessed December 28, 2017. https://www.investors.com/politics/editorials/how-decades-of-democratic-rule-ruined-some-of-our-finest-cities/.

20. Parker, Star. "Back on Uncle Sam's Plantation." Townhall.com. February 9, 2009. Accessed December 28, 2017. https://townhall.com/columnists/starparker/2009/02/09/back-on-uncle-sams-plantation-n1009056.

21. Fisher, Daniel. "The 10 Most Dangerous U.S. Cities." *Forbes*. October 18, 2012. Accessed January 22, 2018. https://www.forbes.com/sites/danielfisher/2012/10/18/detroit-tops-the-2012-list-of-americas-most-dangerous-cities/#23a2b75e2931.

22. Franz, Richard. "Urban America should give up on the Democrats." *The Baltimore Sun*, July 2, 2015. Accessed December 28, 2017. http://www.baltimoresun.com/news/opinion/oped/bs-ed-bad-democrats-20150702-story.html.

23. "Party Breakdown." U.S. House of Representatives Press Gallery. Accessed December 30, 2017. https://pressgallery.house.gov/member-data/party-breakdown.

24. "Party Division." United States Senate. Accessed December 30, 2017. https://www.senate.gov/history/partydiv.htm.

25. "By the numbers: Teachers union political contributions in 2016." FOX News. January 17, 2017. Accessed December 28, 2017. http://www.foxnews.com/politics/2017/01/17/by-numbers-teachers-union-political-contributions-in-2016.html.

26. Walser, Ray. "NEA Doesn't Represent All Teachers." The Heritage Foundation. July 2, 2008. Accessed December 28, 2017. http://www.heritage.org/education/report/nea-doesnt-represent-all-teachers.

27. Goodman, Alana. "National Education Association a Left-Wing 'Lobbying Group.' You'd Never Know it Watching Networks." NewsBusters. Media Research Center. September 29, 2010. Accessed December 28,

2017. https://www.newsbusters.org/articles/national-education-association-left-wing-lobbying-group-youd-never-know-it-watching-network.

28. Kaub, Verne P. *Communist-Socialist Propaganda in American Schools*. 4th ed. Boston, Massachusetts: Meador Publishing Company, 1958.

29. Kaub, *Communist-Socialist Propaganda in American Schools.*

30. Kaub, *Communist-Socialist Propaganda in American Schools.*

Chapter 11
Great Again

On January 19th, 2017, I drove to Washington, D.C. with my daughter Stephanie. We made this four hundred and eighty mile journey because the very next day would mark the most important moment in twenty-first century American history so far.

I believed that then—and I *know* it today. As of January 20th, for the first time since President Theodore Roosevelt—if not longer—the United States has a President who understands the needs and concerns of the working class Little Guy just as much as he understands the responsibilities of Big Business to move our economy forward.

Huddled between twin sisters from North Carolina who both wore "Make America Great Again" hats, I heard President Donald J. Trump with my own ears share his wisdom for a renewed America. Someday, this excerpt of the President's inauguration speech will be set in stone—a monument to the

TOBACCO, TRUSTS, AND TRUMP

man who stood up to the Establishment on behalf of the common man.

> January 20th, 2017 will be remembered as the day the people became the rulers of this nation again.
>
> The forgotten men and women of our country will be forgotten no longer...At the center of this movement is a crucial conviction, that a nation exists to serve its citizens. Americans want great schools for their children, safe neighborhoods for their families, and good jobs for themselves. These are just and reasonable demands of righteous people and a righteous public.
>
> But for too many of our citizens, a different reality exists: mothers and children trapped in poverty in our inner cities; rusted out factories scattered like tombstones across the landscape of our nation; an education system flush with cash, but which leaves our young and beautiful students deprived of all knowledge; and the crime and the gangs and the

drugs that have stolen too many lives and robbed our country of so much unrealized potential.[1]

No informed American can disagree with any of the President's statements. In fact, I guarantee the Leftist media would have eaten it up like pigeons with birdseed if a Democrat had given this speech. Over the course of a few paragraphs, President Trump correctly labeled every symptom of our nation's deepest wounds.

The education system is in shambles, the consequence of teachers who don't actually teach. The neighborhoods I used to ride my bike around as a kid at all hours of the night are now neighborhood watch areas with high crime and even higher addiction rates. Incentivized by high corporate taxes, businesses of all sizes have shipped our jobs overseas in a box labelled "expendable." Uncle Sam's Plantation keeps millions of minority families in our inner cities enslaved in the cycle of generational poverty.

Finally, someone is doing something about it. One year into President Trump's first term (at the time of this writing), America's future is already brighter than it was on January 19th, 2017. During the President's first three months in office, more than half a million new jobs were created.[2] The stock market rally since his inauguration is the second biggest in six decades.[3] Unemployment has fallen

TOBACCO, TRUSTS, AND TRUMP

to nearly four percent, which hasn't been seen since *before* the Great Recession.[4]

According to the Bureau of Labor Statistics, unemployment among African-Americans is the lowest since 1972—not thanks to Ex-President Obama, but thanks to President Trump. As Star Parker writes in *The Gainesville Sun*, "Donald Trump was onto something when he asked blacks, during the presidential campaign, 'What do you have to lose?'"[5]

At the same time, America's Gross Domestic Product (GDP) growth rate, which is used to measure the value of all products and services on the market, increased for two quarters in a row for the first time in three years. More jobs have been created as a result—almost two million new jobs in President Trump's first year in office. Meanwhile, the Dow Jones Industrial Average index hit record highs over sixty times during his early presidency, including an all-time high of twenty-four thousand points. A consequence of this? More than five *trillion* dollars in wealth has been added to our economy since the inauguration. Investors aren't the only guys happy about this—the Consumer Confidence Index rose to a seventeen year high in November 2017.[6]

To drain the habitat of Deep State swamp creatures, the President instituted a five year ban on lobbying for former White House officials.[7] At the same time, the Trump administration has eliminated twenty-two job-killing regulations for every one new regulation, and saved over eight billion dollars in annual regulatory costs.[8]

Our business interests in the Pacific rim are no longer at the whim of other countries that are a fraction of a fraction of our size. The disastrously anti-American Trans-Pacific Partnership has no place in a renewed economy.[9]

The future voting bloc of the Democratic party—illegal aliens who prey on the welfare budget—finally have to answer for their crimes. No city within our borders should be a sanctuary for lawbreakers. How can any sane person think that was a good idea? Already, would-be criminals, drug traffickers, and future Democrats have taken the hint. Between December 2016 and March 2017, illegal immigration plummeted by seventy-two percent.[10] It's astonishing what a President with a backbone can do.

Speaking of a spine, President Trump stood up to the radical environmentalists, signing an Executive Order to expand offshore oil and gas drilling—seventy-seven million acres in the Gulf of Mexico, to be precise. He also approved the Keystone XL and Dakota Access pipelines, which will create approximately forty-two thousand new jobs and two billion dollars in economic benefits.[11]

To protect Americans' safety at home, President Trump's Justice Department announced more than ninety-eight million dollars in grant funding to hire over eight hundred additional full-time law enforcement officers to get the drugs, gangs, and crime off the streets. In 2017 alone, the President spread nearly five hundred million dollars across all fifty states to prevent and treat opioid abuse.[12]

Tax reform closed out 2017, loosening Uncle Sam's grip on America's paychecks.[13] As a result of the Tax Cuts Act, employees at Rumford Industrial Group are each seeing between twenty-five and one hundred dollars more per paycheck.

Thanks to lower taxes across the board, Apple is bringing almost *all* of its two hundred and fifty billion dollars in overseas holdings back to US soil (and banks). According to Apple's website:

> Combining new investments and Apple's current pace of spending with domestic suppliers and manufacturers—an estimated $55 billion for 2018—Apple's direct contribution to the US economy will be more than $350 billion over the next five years, not including Apple's ongoing tax payments, the tax revenues generated from employees' wages and the sale of Apple products.[14]

Apple isn't alone in their commitment. From giant corporations like AT&T, Boeing, and Wells Fargo to small companies all across America, business leaders are investing the first round of new tax savings directly into their people. Four-figure bonuses and hourly wage increases are the post-tax reform norm.[15]

Naturally, the Tax Cuts Act has been defamed by the "quasi-communistic" Left as a corporate handout. But nearly sixty percent of the five and a half *trillion* dollar cuts go to families, not businesses. The average family of four will now save two thousand dollars a year just from the federal income tax decrease.[16]

Thank you, Mr. President.

Because of this "Trump Effect," businesses are hiring, people are working, families are prospering, and investors are creating new opportunities for growth and expansion from sea to shining sea.

The state of the economy is a reflection of the President. Even the Lefties are benefiting from these sensible policies. But there is a problem; popular opinion doesn't reflect all the good that President Trump has promoted, pushed, and made possible. According to a Gallup poll in March 2017, the President's job approval rating collapsed to an unprecedented thirty-six percent.[17] That's even lower than the lowest approval rating of Ex-President Obama during his eight year regime. By December 2017, President Trump hadn't even climbed back up to forty percent. In a SurveyMonkey poll between November 24th and 28th of over fourteen thousand

TOBACCO, TRUSTS, AND TRUMP

Americans—a much larger sample size than Gallup, Rasmussen, and others—President Trump's disapproval rating was a staggering sixty percent.[18]

Does the majority of Americans hate good jobs? Are they okay with criminals running free in the streets? Do they hate bigger paychecks? Are they okay with America getting the short end of the stick in trade deals?

The country is finally being run like a profitable business by a successful businessman, but six out of every ten citizens don't like the Chief Executive responsible for it. I don't think it's because most Americans would rather live in Syria, Iran, or North Korea. Although the Socialists who burn our flag on college campuses during protests are welcome to buy one-way tickets to any of those countries.

The fact is, the vast majority of people support everything that President Donald J. Trump supports. According to Gallup, more than half of Americans think their taxes are too high.[19] I guess the other half are members of the Democratic party, but that's another story.

Gallup also found that, given the choice to receive more public and social services in exchange for higher taxes, only one in five Americans would take Uncle Sam up on the offer.[20] When it comes to illegal immigration and the TPP, the majority of Americans side with the President's views, too. Almost sixty percent of us worry about illegal immi-

GREAT AGAIN

grants sneaking across the border to wreak havoc, according to research also done by Gallup.[21] "Worry" is a strong word.

And of all Americans who actually understood the ramifications of the Trans-Pacific Partnership, the majority opposed it by several percentage points.[22]

The American people agree with President Trump. Why don't they approve of the job he's doing?

It's simple—they don't know about the job he's been doing. The Leftist institutions of Harvard University and *The Washington Post* both admitted that over ninety percent of all mainstream media news coverage of the Trump administration has been negative.[23] That's called media bias.

Pew Research Center compared the number of positive news stories about President Trump to the positive coverage of previous administrations. A shameless forty-two percent of all news stories related to now Ex-President Obama were positive.[24] Not just neutral—*positive*. But for President Trump? Only five percent.

Realize what this means: The majority of Americans *agree* with President Trump; but the majority of Americans *disapprove* of President Trump himself. The mainstream media has collectively refused to tell the American people the truth. That's why "#FakeNews" appears in the President's tweets so often.[25] Just as not telling the whole truth is a form of lying, not reporting the day's real news is a form of fake news.

If you were awake during the past few chapters, you know that the Establishment on the Left has worked to undermine American freedom and prosperity for over one hundred and twenty-five years.

Is it possible that their unofficial propaganda networks—MSNBC, CNN, *Salon*, *The Huffington Post*, and others—have set up the journalist version of a blockade around the Trump administration so no truth gets in or out?

You already know my answer.

At every turn, the Establishment *must* discredit President Trump because his administration is such a threat to their agenda. Not even a year in office, President Trump has taken an axe to the Lefties' orchard and hacked away at the lowest hanging fruit.

With 2017 setting the tone, what do you think *they* think America will look like in 2020 or in 2024 when his daughter Ivanka becomes the first female President? Whatever it is, the Left doesn't want it. What is good for America, is not good for them. So the mainstream media uses their only weapon—dishonesty. They have to portray President Trump as a liar, a racist, a scoundrel, and a cheat every chance they get.

Take the inauguration itself, for example. How Liberal pundits responded to President Trump's account of the viewership tells you everything you need to know about their integrity. While "news" outlets from *Saturday Night Live* to Antifa blogs on Tumblr claimed that the President exaggerated how many people attended his inauguration, I knew the truth—not only because I was there and saw how crowded the Metro was, but because I was proactive about learning the facts! A company called Akamai Technologies—a delivery network for online video and digital content—reported what the mainstream media refused to tell America about the total viewership size.

> Video streaming coverage of the 2017 Presidential Inauguration is the largest single live news event that the company has delivered...[It is] a new benchmark for live video traffic.[26]

But if you watched just thirty seconds of Rachel Maddow, you'd think that only half a Cub Scout troop showed up and that President Trump has dementia! This is more than just revisionist history, it is revisionist *journalism*. Leftists are tearing down statues of American heroes at the same time they're trying to tear down our current President. If you're like me, this incenses you. You cannot believe that they are allowed to get away with this.

Unfortunately, this isn't unusual in American history. Are students taught that thousands of masked men terrorized the midwest and south at the turn of the previous century because of the guy whom Duke University is named after? No. Are students taught the principle of hand-ups and not handouts that Teddy Roosevelt relied on to bring the Trusts to justice while protecting capitalism? No. Are students taught that federal, state, and local governments are behind countless murders of working class people who were simply tired of being taken advantage of? No. What do we see instead? What are textbooks teaching the next generation?

"Christopher Columbus committed genocide."
"Thomas Jefferson was a rapist."
"Robert E. Lee was America's Hitler."

I wish I was exaggerating. The Establishment can't have us knowing that truth.

Because the truth will set America free.

Since the Establishment isn't going to do it, that job is left to us—the American people and public servants like President Trump who represent us. We have to be willing to stand up for the truth when the Establishment does not. And that's going to require more than tweeting our support of the President every day or sharing news from a Conservative perspective on Facebook. There is more work to be done in Congress and on main street, but together, I believe the best is yet to come...if we do the work.

> From now on, America will be empowered by our aspirations, not

GREAT AGAIN

burdened by our fears; inspired by the future, not bound by the failures of the past; and guided by our vision, not blinded by our doubts.[27]

I agree with the President. Do you?

Notes:

1. "Read Donald Trump's Full Inauguration Speech." Time. January 20, 2017. Accessed December 28, 2017. http://time.com/4640707/donald-trump-inauguration-speech-transcript/.

2. Hawkins, John. "The 10 Best Things About Trump's First 100 Days in Office." Townhall.com. August 29, 2017. Accessed December 28, 2017. https://townhall.com/columnists/johnhawkins/2017/04/29/the-10-best-things-about-trumps-first-100-days-in-office-n2320022.

3. Egan, Matt. "Trump rally is 2nd best since JFK." CNN Money. April 28, 2017. Accessed December 28, 2017. http://money.cnn.com/2017/04/28/investing/trump-rally-wall-street-100-days/.

4. Swanson, Ana. "Unemployment rate drops to lowest level in a decade in April as economy adds 211,000 jobs." *The Washington Post*, May 5, 2017. Accessed December 28, 2017. https://www.washingtonpost.com/news/wonk/wp/2017/05/05/the-u-s-job-market-is-expected-to-rebound-in-april-if-it-doesnt-that-could-be-cause-for-concern/?utm_term=.91d745106989.

5. Parker, Star. "Parker: Trump can take credit for drop in black unemployment." *The Gainesville Sun*. January 22, 2018. Accessed January 22, 2018. http://www.gainesville.com/opinion/20180122/parker-trump-can-take-credit-for-drop-in-black-unemployment.

6. "President Donald J. Trump: Year One of Making America Great Again." WhiteHouse.gov. December 22, 2017. Accessed January 22, 2018. https://www.whitehouse.gov/briefings-statements/president-donald-j-trump-year-one-making-america-great/?utm_source=link.

7. Hawkins, "The 10 Best Things About Trump's First 100

TOBACCO, TRUSTS, AND TRUMP

Days in Office."

8. "President Donald J. Trump: Year One of Making America Great Again." WhiteHouse.gov. December 22, 2017. Accessed January 22, 2018. https://www.whitehouse.gov/briefings-statements/president-donald-j-trump-year-one-making-america-great/?utm_source=link.

9. Hawkins, "The 10 Best Things About Trump's First 100 Days in Office."

10. Garcia, Carlos. "Illegal border crossings plummet to lowest in 17 years, Trump rhetoric credited." The Blaze. April 4, 2017. Accessed December 28, 2017. http://www.theblaze.com/news/2017/04/04/illegal-border-crossings-plummet-to-lowest-in-17-years-trump-rhetoric-credited.

11. "President Donald J. Trump: Year One of Making America Great Again." WhiteHouse.gov. December 22, 2017. Accessed January 22, 2018. https://www.whitehouse.gov/briefings-statements/president-donald-j-trump-year-one-making-america-great/?utm_source=link.

12. "President Donald J. Trump: Year One of Making America Great Again." WhiteHouse.gov. December 22, 2017. Accessed January 22, 2018. https://www.whitehouse.gov/briefings-statements/president-donald-j-trump-year-one-making-america-great/?utm_source=link.

13. Chakraborty, Barnini. "Trump signs tax overhaul, budget bill before heading to Mar-a-Lago." FOX News. December 22, 2017. Accessed December 28, 2017. http://www.foxnews.com/politics/2017/12/22/trump-signs-tax-overhaul-budget-bill-before-heading-to-mar-lago.html.

14. Erb, Kelly Phillips. "Apple Says It Will Bring Cash Back To U.S., Pay $38 Billion In Repatriation Tax." Forbes. January 17, 2018. https://www.forbes.com/sites/kellyphillipserb/2018/01/17/apple-says-it-will-bring-cash-back-to-us-pay-38-billion-in-repatriation-tax/#6dc9be9d2222.

15. "Bonuses, minimum wage hikes: how some big businesses react to tax cut." WCVB Boston. Updated December 20, 2017. Accessed January 22, 2018. http://www.wcvb.com/article/bonuses-minimum-wage-hikes-how-some-big-businesses-react-to-tax-cut/14474321.

16. "President Donald J. Trump: Year One of Making America Great Again." WhiteHouse.gov. December 22, 2017. Accessed January 22, 2018. https://www.whitehouse.gov/briefings-statements/president-donald-j-trump-

year-one-making-america-great/?utm_source=link.

17. Newport, Frank. "Trump's Approval Rating Drops to New Low of 36%." Gallup News. March 27, 2017. Accessed December 28, 2017. http://news.gallup.com/opinion/polling-matters/207416/trump-approval-rating-drops-new-low.aspx.

18. Bycoffe, Aaron, Dhrumil Mehta, and Nate Silver. "How Popular Is Donald Trump?" FiveThirtyEight. Updated December 28, 2017. Accessed December 28, 2017. https://projects.fivethirtyeight.com/trump-approval-ratings/?ex_cid=rrpromo.

19. "Taxes." Gallup Historical Trends. Gallup News. Accessed December 28, 2017. http://news.gallup.com/poll/1714/taxes.aspx.

20. "Taxes," Gallup News.

21. Jones, Jeffrey M. "In U.S., Worry About Illegal Immigration Steady." Gallup News. March 20, 2017. Accessed December 28, 2017. http://news.gallup.com/poll/206681/worry-illegal-immigration-steady.aspx.

22. Trump, Donald J. "Presidential Memorandum Regarding Withdrawal of the United States from the Trans-Pacific Partnership Negotiations and Agreement." The White House. January 23, 2017. Accessed December 28, 2017. https://www.whitehouse.gov/presidential-actions/presidential-memorandum-regarding-withdrawal-united-states-trans-pacific-partnership-negotiations-agreement/.

23. Wemple, Erik. "Study: 91 percent of recent network Trump coverage has been negative." *The Washington Post*, September 12, 2017. Accessed December 28, 2017. https://www.washingtonpost.com/blogs/erik-wemple/wp/2017/09/12/study-91-percent-of-recent-network-trump-coverage-has-been-negative/?utm_term=.8a65b5ced708.

24. Kurtzleben, Danielle. "Study: News Coverage Of Trump More Negative Than For Other Presidents." NPR. October 2, 2017. Accessed December 28, 2017. https://www.npr.org/2017/10/02/555092743/study-news-coverage-of-trump-more-negative-than-for-other-presidents.

25. Szathmary, Zoe, and Alex Pappas. "'Stain on America!' Trump denounces 'Fake News Media' after string of major reporting errors exposed." FOX News. December 10, 2017. Accessed December 30, 2017. http://www.foxnews.com/politics/2017/12/10/stain-on-america-trump-de-

nounces-fake-news-media-after-string-major-reporting-errors-exposed.html.

26. Harper, Jennifer. "Victory in live video streaming: Trump inauguration drew record online audiences." *The Washington Times*. January 22, 2017. Accessed December 28, 2017. https://www.washingtontimes.com/news/2017/jan/22/donald-trump-inauguration-drew-record-online-audie/.

27. "President Donald J. Trump: Year One of Making America Great Again." WhiteHouse.gov. December 22, 2017. Accessed January 22, 2018.

Chapter 12
More Work to Be Done

In 2013, the Bullitt County History Museum of Shepherdsville, Kentucky was gifted a copy of an original 1912 eighth grade test.[1] In those days, graduating the eighth grade was the equivalent of graduating high school, so earning a passing grade on that test was a big deal. When the copy of the test was published online, the Bullitt County History Museum received hundreds of thousands of hits. Pictures of the test then went viral on social media because the questions stumped adults!

For example, the Geography section asked students to define latitude and longitude. Can you do that without Googling them?

In the Arithmetic section, students are asked to calculate compound interest accumulated over the course of three years, three months, and three days. Can you get the answer without using a calculator? Can you get it *with* a calculator?

TOBACCO, TRUSTS, AND TRUMP

On Civil Government, students are asked to compare and contrast copyrights and patent rights. Did you know that there is even a difference between the two?

I'll admit it, these questions stumped me, too. But the reemergence of that 1912 test should be interpreted as more than an oddity to make fun of your co-workers because they don't know where the Erie Canal was or why President Andrew Johnson was impeached.

The fact is, many schools within the American education system have sharply declined in quality since the early twentieth century, and we are paying the price today. Fortunately, great school systems do exist in the United States. Oakwood City School District, for example, consistently sees ninety-nine percent of students graduate, who go on to even greater successes in their careers and lives.[2] Other cities in the Miami Valley boast high school gradu-ation rates above ninety-seven percent, including Bellbrook, Centerville, and Springboro.[3,4,5] If only inner city schools held themselves to such high standards; graduation rates in Baltimore, Chicago, and Detroit sit at seventy-three, seventy-three, and seventy-eight percent respectively.[6,7,8] And nationally, as of 2015, our students' tests scores put us twenty-fourth in the world in science, thirty-eighth in mathematics, and twenty-fourth in reading.[9] In science and reading, those scores define America's

MORE WORK TO BE DONE

youth as barely above average. It's even worse in mathematics, where students' test scores put them below average compared to other countries.

In 1630, Governor John Winthrop of the Massachusetts colony proclaimed America's destiny as a city upon a hill—the eyes of all people are upon us.[10] If that statement is true, then all people should not like what they see when they look at our education system. In that case, we're a city in a sewer.

My research has shown that several factors have led to that decline—although there are ways to fix it. President Donald J. Trump has already put one solution into play in the person of Betsy DeVos, the Secretary of Education (more on her later).

First of all, when I was a youngster, we were allowed to roam the woods, wade in the school side creek, and play dodgeball during recess. We had the freedom to just be kids when it wasn't time to learn. When it was time to learn, our teachers used discipline to make sure we did. It's a shame rulers for unruly kids' knuckles have been replaced by Adderall, Ritalin, and other drugs that turn kids into zombies.

When you use drugs to change the way kids think and behave, don't be surprised if you fundamentally change the way they learn, too. Of course, the Lefties in academia think the childhood urges to run, jump, and play should be permanently suppressed. That makes it easier to load their brains up with all sorts of nonsense about the "pros" of communism, so-called "white privilege," and the "evils" of patriarchy. In other words, kids these days are learning so much BS that they don't actually learn anything useful! Then when they go off to college, the non-learning continues.

That's our second problem. The fact that forty-eight percent of Americans with a college degree are working in a career that didn't require a degree should tell us all something.[11] What the hell are college students doing for four or more years? They aren't learning employable skills, that's for sure. But at the same time, the cost of a college degree has increased by a factor of twelve since the 1970's.[12]

After World War II, the United States saw a rush to colleges and universities that had never been seen before in the history of the world. After the G.I. Bill, officially known as the Servicemen's Readjustment Act of 1944, over two million soldiers used the bill's benefits to go to college over the next decade.[13] What does the Greatest Generation tell their kids the Baby Boomers, who then tell their kids Generation X and Generation Y? *"Go to college and get a degree."*

Federal subsidies triggered an increase of the price (because everyone wanted one), a drop off of the quality (because learning institutions became diploma mills), and a decrease of the inherent value of a degree (because so many people have them). When I reached my eighteenth birthday, maybe

MORE WORK TO BE DONE

five or six out of every hundred people had a college degree. Today, more than a third of all Americans over twenty-five have one.[14]

Dramatic demographic shifts have dramatic consequences, and they are showing up in the decline of America's standing in the world. Fortunately, there are solutions, and President Trump has been pointing them out. When then-Candidate Trump campaigned across the midwest in 2016, he made a habit out of visiting manufacturers, machine shops, and technology-driven assembly lines. The United States became the world's first great superpower because our manufacturing companies were second to none. You can thank the World War II effort for that. Our industrial sector wasn't destroyed by war.

With ten thousand Baby Boomers retiring every day, and many of them from blue collar jobs, we have a widening gap between the degrees Americans have and the available careers there actually are.

There are over six hundred thousand open jobs in America's manufacturing sector right now.[15] But thanks to Leftist indoctrination about the need for a degree, twentysomethings are going to public universities to get degrees in LGBT studies instead of a trade school for a certificate.

For roughly two thousand dollars to earn a professional certificate and four thousand dollars for an associate's degree, a young person can acquire the technical skills that make them the perfect candi-

TOBACCO, TRUSTS, AND TRUMP

date for stable, salaried careers.[16,17] This viable career path allows people to take a detour around Liberal college professors who are flower children of the 1960's—former Vietnam war protesters and pro-Soviet draft dodgers.

In Dayton, Ohio, the Patterson Co-Op was a high school named after John H. Patterson. This high school taught kids technical skills and offered apprenticeships sponsored by local manufacturers. These apprenticeships lead directly to full-time employment in stable careers.[18] Because of their success in creating employment opportunities and helping the economy grow, other educators and businesses joined together throughout the twentieth century to launch more co-ops. I even became a professor at one, teaching welding and metallurgy.

By highlighting both the challenges and opportunities of blue collar America, President Trump is pointing the next generation in the direction of viable career paths that can give Americans the technical skills they need to raise us out of educational mediocrity.[19,20] Of course, Leftist educators hate the President for this. They harass and defame his Secretary of Education Betsy DeVos because she has very little experience in public education.[21] Have they ever thought that maybe that's the point?

The path through Liberal colleges that once seemed like a requirement to get a good job has become one of many options. Instead, students can choose a trade school, vocational school, or community college that offers a shorter, less expensive path to a good career. Whatever Secretary DeVos can do to weaken the power of the Department of Education, the Marxist National Education Association, and the Establishment as a whole, I am for it!

While we're at it, we have to free the slaves from Uncle Sam's Plantation—the poverty cycle that keeps women locked into a hopeless and helpless reliance on government handouts. One of the few who got out, Star Parker founded the Center for Urban Renewal and Education (CURE) to help fellow women and minorities cut the cord of welfare dependence and take responsibility for their own families, careers, and lives.[22] Star's organization sure has their work cut out for them; when Star herself got caught for shoplifting at twelve years old, her school's guidance counselor excused away her behavior as the result of "victimhood." Because Star is black, she is supposedly powerless against an oppressive, racist society.[23] How many more misguided "guidance" counselors like Star Parker's are there are out there?

I've always said that ninety percent of Americans are not racist, so I want to be careful how I address the issue of race and poverty. Instead of making it all about the color of people's skin like the Lefties do with that"Identity Politics" BS, I want to focus on the facts. And one of the most troubling facts about black families today is that seventy-two percent of all African-Americans are born to single mothers.[24] Just about every social problem we deal with today, from emotional disorders to financial problems, are directly correlated with single parent families.[25,26]

Blame that on President Lyndon B. Johnson, the most Socialist President we've ever had (yet). His administration's "war on poverty" has only made things worse.[27] Men and women have traded a stable family for single parenthood and child support. Fast forward from the 1960's to 2014, and only twenty-nine percent of African-Americans were married, compared to forty-eight percent of Americans overall.[28]

Without two parents working to build a better future for their children, the family suffers. White families on average have a net worth that is ten times higher than black families.[29] I don't blame this on racism—except on the racism of Leftist Progressives who have unfairly targeted blacks and other racial minorities in order to make them a permanent voting bloc. The Democrats are trying to do the same thing with illegal immigrants, opening up federal welfare and voting rights to them despite the laws they have broken or their employment status.[30,31,32]

That's why the Lefties lost what little bit of their minds they had left when President Trump signed an Executive Order on May 11, 2017, which created the Presidential Advisory Commission on Election

MORE WORK TO BE DONE

Integrity.[33] Unless Democrats create new voters out of thin air—or by giving illegal immigrants the right to vote—they are not going to have the upper hand in future elections.

I hope to God they never do. With how things are going, it looks like they never will. President Trump's decision to nominate renowned neurosurgeon Dr. Ben Carson as the Secretary of Housing and Urban Development (HUD) shows that the days of Uncle Sam's Plantation are numbered.

The son of a single mother who worked as a housekeeper, Dr. Carson proved that the institutionalized racism of the Reconstruction era does not exist in modern society. Instead of turning him and his brother over to the streets and their drugs, crime, and gangs, his mother instilled within them a work ethic and a desire to better themselves. Now that Dr. Carson oversees HUD, he has the opportunity to share that lesson with the tens of millions who find themselves enslaved within a cycle of generational poverty enforced by Leftist policies.[34]

One of the fastest ways to create a work ethic is to take away handouts, which President Trump's 2017 federal budget does. At the time of this writing, the HUD budget is set to be slashed by thirteen percent in 2018, roughly six billion dollars.[35]

Rather than keep the urban poor suffering on the streets, barely making it by with handouts, Dr.

TOBACCO, TRUSTS, AND TRUMP

Carson intends to offer people a path out of poverty through self-generated initiative and personal responsibility:

> We take the homeless and we put them in a shelter, number one. Number two, we diagnose why they're there. And number three, we fix it... [T]hat's what's being really compassionate.[36]

After auditing HUD, Dr. Carson and his team uncovered over five hundred *billion* dollars worth of errors as a result of the Obama administration's "inability to establish a compliant control environment, implement adequate financial accounting systems, retain key financial staff, and identify appropriate accounting principles and policies."[37] It turns out that running government programs like a business saves taxpayer dollars and gets results.

Free the slaves.

Climbing back to the top of John Winthrop's hill starts with solving our nation's worst problems, and the learning ethic and work ethic are two of them. As you can see, we are already beginning to make progress thanks to President Trump and his team of swamp-drainers. The future is bright, as many of American history's wrongs outlined in

MORE WORK TO BE DONE

the preceding chapters of this book are now being righted. But there is more work to be done—and you can roll up your sleeves to help. If you have children, teenagers, or young adults in your life, point them to those more than half a million open jobs. Talk about the three trillion-dollar student loan debt crisis, which cripples Millennials financially so they can't afford homes, families, or vacations that young professionals in past generations could.[38]

And if you know families who are stuck in generational poverty or are hunkering down inside the war zones of the inner city, tell them the good news of hand-ups like free career coaching and resume writing services offered by nonprofits and the education grants that are available to low-income families.

America is the greatest country in the world for making something of your life. Conservatives can stand on American Exceptionalism. The fact is, forty percent of Fortune 500 companies in the United States were started by immigrants or the children of immigrants.[39] If you have a will to learn and a will to work, you can become anything in this country, whether you are a Kentucky tobacco farmer like me or a millionaire turned billionaire who became President.

This is the land of opportunities. Let's keep it that way—and create more of them.

TOBACCO, TRUSTS, AND TRUMP

Notes:

1. Sieczkowski, Cavan. "1912 Eighth-Grade Exam Stumps 21st-Century Test-Takers." The Huffington Post. August 12, 2013. Accessed December 28, 2017. https://www.huffingtonpost.com/2013/08/12/1912-eighth-grade-exam_n_3744163.html.

2. "Oakwood High School." Public School Review. Accessed January 8, 2018. https://www.publicschoolreview.com/oakwood-high-school-profile/45419.

3. "Bellbrook High School." U.S. News & World Report. Accessed February 12, 2018. https://www.usnews.com/education/best-high-schools/ohio/districts/bellbrook-sugar-creek-local-school-district/bellbrook-high-school-15537.

4. "Centerville High School." Public School Review. Accessed February 12, 2018. https://www.publicschoolreview.com/centerville-high-school-profile/45459.

5. "Springboro High School." U.S. News & World Report. Accessed February 12, 2018. https://www.usnews.com/education/best-high-schools/ohio/districts/springboro-community-city/springboro-high-school-15775.

6. Campbell, Colin. "Graduation rates at city schools below average, but rising." *The Baltimore Sun*, December 16, 2014. Accessed February 12, 2018. http://www.baltimoresun.com/news/maryland/baltimore-city/bs-md-ci-graduation-rate-20141216-story.html.

7. Perez, Juan, Jr., and Kyle Bentle. "Data: Chicago Public Schools touts improved graduation rate." *The Chicago Tribune*, September 5, 2016. Accessed February 12, 2018. http://www.chicagotribune.com/news/ct-chicago-schools-graduation-rates-20160905-htmlstory.html.

8. Leeds, Lauren. "Statewide Graduation and Dropout Rates Show Little Change. Graduation Rate Remains at 79 Percent." State of Michigan. Accessed February 12, 2018. http://www.michigan.gov/som/0,4669,7-192-26847-407443--,00.html.

9. DeSilver, Drew. "U.S. students' academic achievement still lags that of their peers in many other countries." Pew Research Center. February 15, 2017. Accessed December 28, 2017. http://www.pewresearch.org/fact-tank/2017/02/15/u-s-students-internationally-math-science/.

10. Winthrop, John. *A Modell of Christian Charity*. Collections of the Massachusetts Historical Society, 3rd ser. (1838). Hanover Historical Texts Collection. (August 1996). Accessed December 28, 2017. https://history.hanover.edu/texts/winthmod.html.

MORE WORK TO BE DONE

11. Adams, Susan. "Half Of College Grads Are Working Jobs That Don't Require A Degree." *Forbes*. May 28, 2013. Accessed December 28, 2017. https://www.forbes.com/sites/susanadams/2013/05/28/half-of-college-grads-are-working-jobs-that-dont-require-a-degree/#21a41ba96d7a.

12. Jamrisko, Michelle, and Ilan Kolet. "Cost of College Degree in U.S. Soars 12 Fold: Chart of the Day." Bloomberg. August 15, 2012. Accessed December 28, 2017. https://www.bloomberg.com/news/articles/2012-08-15/cost-of-college-degree-in-u-s-soars-12-fold-chart-of-the-day.

13. Bound, John, and Sarah Turner. "Going to War and Going to College: Did World War II and the G.I. Bill Increase Educational Attainment for Returning Veterans?" *Journal of Labor Economics* 20, no. 4 (2002): 784-815.

14. Wilson, Reid. "Census: More Americans have college degrees than ever before." The Hill. April 3, 2017. Accessed December 28, 2017. http://thehill.com/homenews/statewatch/326995-census-more-americans-have-college-degrees-than-ever-before.

15. Smith, Casey. "Dream It Do It celebrates young manufacturers, kicks off 2015 campaign." *Tulsa World*, August 12, 2015. Accessed December 28, 2017. http://www.tulsaworld.com/business/manufacturing/dream-it-do-it-celebrates-young-manufacturers-kicks-off-campaign/article_0b6b61df-521e-526f-8846-610f77c8e48b.html.

16. "Current Tuition Cost and Fee Schedule." Sinclair College. Accessed December 28, 2017. https://www.sinclair.edu/services/basics/bursar/tuition-fee-schedule/.

17. "Undergraduate certificate in Computer Aided Manufacturing/Precision Machining Short Term Certificate (CAMPM.S.STC),GainfulEmploymentDisclosure."Sinclair College. June 19, 2017. Accessed December 28, 2017. http://apps.sinclair.edu/gainful-employment/CAMPM.S.STC/GEDT.html?_ga=2.229669532.1451485505.1513986780-46543174.1513986780.

18. "High School a Different Way: Learning While Earning." *Dayton, USA*, January 1965. Accessed December 28, 2017. http://www.daytonhistorybooks.com/page/page/4696426.htm.

19. Hughes, Neil. "Apple will bring 3 manufacturing plants to US, President Trump reveals." AppleInsider. July 25, 2017. Accessed December 28, 2017. http://appleinsider.com/articles/17/07/25/apple-will-bring-3-manufacturing-plants-to-us-president-trump-reveals.

20. Miller, S.A. "Blue-collar voters in Democratic strongholds blame Washington establishment, not Trump." *The Wash-*

TOBACCO, TRUSTS, AND TRUMP

ington Times. July 19, 2017. Accessed December 28, 2017. https://www.washingtontimes.com/news/2017/jul/19/donald-trumps-blue-collar-support-still-strong-in-/.

21. "Why is Betsy DeVos, Trump's pick for education secretary, so unpopular?" BBC News. February 7, 2017. Accessed December 28, 2017. http://www.bbc.com/news/world-us-canada-38875924.

22. "Star Parker - CURE." CURE. Accessed January 22, 2018. https://www.urbancure.org/star-parker.

23. Cruz, Suzanne. "If You Don't Know Star Parker, You Should." Fairfax Free Citizen. October 31, 2017. Accessed January 22, 2018. https://fairfaxfreecitizen.com/2017/10/31/dont-know-star-parker/.

24. Jacobson, Louis. "CNN's Don Lemon says more than 72 percent of African-American births are out of wedlock." PolitiFact. July 29, 2013. Accessed December 28, 2017. http://www.politifact.com/truth-o-meter/statements/2013/jul/29/don-lemon/cnns-don-lemon-says-more-72-percent-african-americ/.

25. Amato, Paul R., Sarah Patterson, and Brett Beattie. "Single-Parent Households and Children's Educational Achievement: A State-Level Analysis." *Social Science Research* 53 (September 2015): 191-202. June 3, 2015. Accessed December 28, 2017. doi:10.1016/j.ssresearch.2015.05.012.

26. Beckford, Martin. "Children in single-parent families more likely to suffer emotional problems, report finds." *The Telegraph*. October 21, 2008. Accessed December 28, 2017. http://www.telegraph.co.uk/news/politics/3235650/Children-in-single-parent-families-more-likely-to-suffer-emotional-problems-report-finds.html.

27. Woodhill, Louis. "The War on Poverty Wasn't A Failure -- It Was A Catastrophe." *Forbes*. March 19, 2014. Accessed December 28, 2017. https://www.forbes.com/sites/louiswoodhill/2014/03/19/the-war-on-poverty-wasnt-a-failure-it-was-a-catastrophe/#7e7226fb6f49.

28. "Marriage in Black America." Black Demographics. Accessed December 28, 2017. http://blackdemographics.com/households/marriage-in-black-america/.

29. Jan, Tracy. "White families have nearly 10 times the net worth of black families. And the gap is growing." *The Washington Post*, September 28, 2017. Accessed December 28, 2017. https://www.washingtonpost.com/news/wonk/wp/2017/09/28/black-and-hispanic-families-are-making-more-money-but-they-still-lag-far-behind-whites/.

30. Mikelionis, Lukas. "Illegal immigrants get OK to vote in Maryland city's elections." FOX News. September 13,

MORE WORK TO BE DONE

2017. Accessed December 28, 2017. http://www.foxnews.com/us/2017/09/13/illegal-immigrants-get-ok-to-vote-in-maryland-citys-elections.html.

31. Edsall, Thomas B. "The Democrats' Immigration Problem." *The New York Times*, February 16, 2017. Accessed December 28, 2017. https://www.nytimes.com/2017/02/16/opinion/the-democrats-immigration-problem.html.

32. Beinart, Peter. "How the Democrats Lost Their Way on Immigration." *The Atlantic*, July/August 2017. Accessed December 28, 2017. https://www.theatlantic.com/magazine/archive/2017/07/the-democrats-immigration-mistake/528678/.

33. "Presidential Advisory Commission on Election Integrity." The White House. July 13, 2017. Accessed December 28, 2017. https://www.whitehouse.gov/articles/presidential-advisory-commission-election-integrity/.

34. "Ben Carson Biography.com." The Biography.com website. Updated March 2, 2017. Accessed December 28, 2017. https://www.biography.com/people/ben-carson-475422.

35. DelReal, Jose A. "Trump budget asks for $6 billion in HUD cuts, drops development grants." *The Washington Post*, March 16, 2017. Accessed December 28, 2017. https://www.washingtonpost.com/politics/trump-budget-asks-for-6-billion-in-hud-cuts-drops-development-grants/2017/03/15/1b157338-09a0-11e7-b77c-0047d15a24e0_story.html?utm_term=.56c30fbba36a.

36. Schwartz, Ian. " Back to Videos HUD's Ben Carson: Running Things In A Businesslike Manner Saves Enormous Amounts Of Money." RealClearPolitics. June 27, 2017. Accessed January 22, 2018. https://www.realclearpolitics.com/video/2017/06/27/huds_ben_carson_running_things_in_a_businesslike_manner_saves_enormous_amounts_of_money.html.

37. Curl, Joseph. "Ben Carson Finds $500 Billion (Billion!) In Errors During Audit Of Obama HUD." The Daily Wire. April 6, 2017. Accessed January 22, 2018. https://www.dailywire.com/news/15163/ben-carson-finds-500-billion-billion-errors-during-joseph-curl#.

38. Friedman, Zack. "Student Loan Debt In 2017: A $1.3 Trillion Crisis." *Forbes*. February 21, 2017. Accessed December 28, 2017. https://www.forbes.com/sites/zackfriedman/2017/02/21/student-loan-debt-statistics-2017/#1ee43b0a5dab.

39. Leadem, Rose. "The Immigrant Entrepreneurs Behind Major American Companies (Infographic)." Entrepreneur. February 4, 2017. Accessed December 28, 2017. https://www.entrepreneur.com/article/288687.

Conclusion
What's the Future?

"History is nothing more than a line of dominoes. Every historical event is both the cause of and result of some other event."

That's not a quote from someone famous, but it should be. Because it's true. This book is proof. The 2016 Presidential Election and the policies of the Trump administration are the result of decades of a Leftist Establishment punishing the middle class work ethic, forcing Socialist propaganda into kids' heads, and taxing both businesses and workers out of prosperity.

Leftist policies, from handouts with a catch to crippling high income taxes, are the result of false promises made to workers during populist uprisings in the late nineteenth and early twentieth century. Those early populist uprisings, like the Tobacco Wars, bank runs, and industrial strikes, were themselves the result of Trust tycoons who sought profit at any price.

WHAT'S THE FUTURE?

In 1904, the Night Riders protested Buck Duke and the Tobacco Trust by setting fire to tobacco warehouses. In 2016, the American people protested the Establishment and Leftist policies by setting fire to the ballot box.

What happened then is the cause of what happens now; what happens now is the cause of what happens in the future. That future—our future—is in your hands.

I think this is why so much of the history revealed in this book has been hidden from the public. The Establishment determines what kids learn in school, so why would they want Americans to learn at an early age that the Establishment is behind everything we've had to deal with for over a hundred years?

In the wake of economic and humanitarian crises between the Civil War and World War I, the Lefties rode into town, promised Americans the world, and sold us a bill of goods we've been paying for ever since. But now you know the truth. What are you going to do with it?

As for me, I decided to write this book. But that's not all. Several summers ago, I was walking my dog around the neighborhood when I saw two young girls selling cups of homemade lemonade on their parents' front lawn.

"I'll take one!" I told them. I reached into my wallet for a crisp dollar bill. "Keep the change."

TOBACCO, TRUSTS, AND TRUMP

They were so excited for what was probably their first sale of the day that they spilled half the cup all over each other. Once they got their act together and fulfilled my order, I asked a question. "Has anyone ever told you about capitalism and entrepreneurship? Because that's what you're doing right now."

They looked at each other, then back at me, then back at each other, and said, "No. What's that?"

I raised my cup of lemonade. "This. Right here. You took some money out of your piggy bank to buy supplies so you could sell lemonade. Then when a customer like me comes along, they pay for the lemonade because they want some. As you sell more and more lemonade, you have extra money to invest in other things. As you help more people and get rewarded for it, you can help even more. That's capitalism. You are both entrepreneurs."

Their wrinkled up noses told me they didn't quite get it, but all I needed to do was plant a seed of interest in the free market.

Last Halloween, my daughter Stephanie and I passed out candy to the neighborhood kids. Dressed as a pair of witches, those two girls—now teenagers—came up to my door.

Hey, look!" They pointed at me and looked at their parents, who stood on the sidewalk "It's the man who taught us about capitalism and entrepreneurship!"

WHAT'S THE FUTURE?

The seed is blossoming. If those sisters ever start a business someday and need investors, I will be the first to put money down.

The Leftist Establishment may be able to tempt Americans with propaganda about fairness, justice, and equal outcomes, but nothing compels people like freedom does—pure, unadulterated, one hundred percent American freedom.

From sending tobacco to auction in Kentucky to selling cups of lemonade in the suburbs, the greatest lesson we can teach the next generation is that sales-driven entrepreneurship in a capitalist economy sets us free. This is what true Progress looks like—the kind President Teddy Roosevelt envisioned for us over a hundred years ago.

As the economy marches forward, technology disrupts industries, and automation changes jobs more drastically than the computer did, capitalism and entrepreneurship are the only things that can keep us on the road to Progress. Any freedom we enjoy along the way will exist because we fought for it—and won. Throughout history, there have always been authoritarians who thought they knew better than the common person, that they could control individuals' lives better than they could.

Napoleon conquered Europe but got his butt kicked by the Russians. The Muslim pirates raped, pillaged, and plundered American ships in the Atlantic and Mediterranean until the United States

TOBACCO, TRUSTS, AND TRUMP

Navy sunk their boats. In the twentieth century, the Kaiser, Hitler, Mussolini, and Stalin all tried to rule their people from the top down. Authoritarians always lose; victory always has a high price tag.

In the United States, Leftist Progressives have shown more and more since the Tobacco Wars that they're willing to follow in the footsteps of authoritarians. It may have started with taxes and economic planning, but where will it end?

I'll tell you where—wherever we, the free people of the United States, decide it ends. The Declaration of Independence, the Constitution, and the Bill of Rights are on our side. The greatest documents in human history guarantee freedom. But we have to fight for it. The 2016 Presidential Election is a battle that freedom won, but the war is far from over.

At the Constitutional Convention, Benjamin Franklin was asked what kind of government he and the other Founding Fathers had designed. "A Republic, if you can keep it," he replied.[1]

It seems appropriate to paraphrase his answer.

"Freedom...if you can keep it."

I'll do my best.

Will you?

Notes:

1. McManus, John F. "A Republic, if You Can Keep It." *The New American*. November 6, 2000. Accessed December 30, 2017. https://www.thenewamerican.com/usnews/constitution/item/7631-a-republic-if-you-can-keep-it.

ABOUT THE AUTHOR

Jim Rumford is an entrepreneur, amateur historian, and CEO of Rumford Industrial Group.

During the Tobacco Wars, Rumford's own Great-Grandfather George Washington Kinney was attacked by "Night Riders," who also burned down the family tobacco barns and destroyed the tobacco crop. To help prevent history from ever repeating itself, Kinney compiled one of the largest private collections of Tobacco Wars primary documents in the United States. At six years old, Rumford discovered these documents and has been telling his Great-Grandfather's story ever since.

TOBACCO, TRUSTS, AND TRUMP

Part memoir, part history, and part warning, Rumford's first book, Tobacco, Trusts, and Trump: How America's Forgotten War Created Big Government, draws startling parallels between the causes and consequences of the Tobacco Wars, and America's political and economic challenges in the Age of Trump.

Born in Louisville, Kentucky, Rumford grew up in Bracken County, Kentucky, and Cincinnati, Ohio, and now resides in Dayton, Ohio.

Learn more about Jim Rumford and *Tobacco, Trusts, and Trump* at www.TheTobaccoWars.com.

www.ingramcontent.com/pod-product-compliance
Lightning Source LLC
Chambersburg PA
CBHW020414080526
44584CB00014B/1321